Getting Naked Later

KATE HURLEY

HARVEST HOUSE PUBLISHERS
EUGENE, OREGON

Cover by Faceout Studios

Cover art by Tim Green/Faceout Studios

Interior design by Rockwell Davis

Published in association with the literary agency of WordServe Literary Group, Ltd., www.word serveliterary.com.

Getting Naked Later
Previously published as *Cupid Is a Procrastinator*
Copyright © 2013 by Kate Hurley
Published by Harvest House Publishers
Eugene, Oregon 97408
www.harvesthousepublishers.com

ISBN 978-0-7369-7833-0 (pbk.)
ISBN 978-0-7369-7834-7 (eBook)

Library of Congress Cataloging-in-Publication Data

Names: Hurley, Kate, 1975- author.
Title: Getting naked later : making sense of the unexpected single life /
    Kate Hurley.
Other titles: Cupid is a procrastinator
Description: Eugene, Oregon : Harvest House Publishers, 2020. | Includes
    bibliographical references. | Summary: "If you're dating, waiting, and
    feeling frustrated, Kate Hurley will help you navigate the path of
    singleness as you grieve your unmet expectations and learn to open your
    heart and life to the unforeseen possibilities of a different kind of
    love story"-- Provided by publisher.
Identifiers: LCCN 2019060178 (print) | LCCN 2019060179 (ebook) | ISBN
    9780736978330 (paperback) | ISBN 9780736978347 (ebook)
Subjects: LCSH: Single people--Religious life. | Christian women--Religious
    life.
Classification: LCC BV4596.S5 H87 2020 (print) | LCC BV4596.S5 (ebook) |
    DDC 248.8086/52--dc23
LC record available at https://lccn.loc.gov/2019060178
LC ebook record available at https://lccn.loc.gov/2019060179

Printed in the United States of America

20 21 22 23 24 25 26 27 / BP-RD / 10 9 8 7 6 5 4 3 2 1

Contents

Foreword

If someone had told me in my twenties that I'd still be waiting on marriage and kids in my fifties, I would have properly rebuked them. But as the decades passed, I had to stumble along the unbeaten path and figure out how to embrace the goodness of God amid unfulfilled desires. I did that by surrounding myself with others who were aimlessly trying to make sense of singleness too.

As I read this book, I wished I'd known Kate Hurley sooner. She has given this generation an indispensable gift. She offers a humble and bold kind of insight for the Christian single who desires marriage.

Kate shares her heart in a way that will melt yours. I especially love how she makes you feel seen and understood as she accurately highlights how our faith is challenged by our circumstances. She draws us in with her humor and poignant experiences and leaves us with a longing to know God more. She helps us see a God who pursues us, cries with us, and is present with us during some of the most confusing and disappointing years. You know she has pored over Scripture for personal revelation as she teaches biblical truths that bring a deeper understanding of the love of God.

She shows us her deep longing for a mate, her fear of never being a mom, her willingness to wrestle with God, and her temptation to throw pity parties. And she even reveals her must-have-in-a-mate list! Because she writes with such vulnerability and authenticity, I found myself unable to put the book down until I knew how she met with God through one of the episodes that resembled something out of *Friends*.

Take the title of this book, for instance. *Getting Naked Later* reminds us that she is not afraid to go where others have been unwilling to go before. She addresses the fallacies of courtship, the chemistry in attraction, and the realities of marriage. You will walk away feeling as though she read your journal and gave you the best big sister advice. Instead of avoiding the tough topics, she dives in and addresses the frustrations of living a prolonged single life. She falls on her sword and reveals the raw details of personal mishaps but always comes back to the confidence she found in Jesus.

Even if you feel you've missed your best dating years, the message in the pages of this book will remind you that God is faithful, his plans are as good as he is, and there is abundant life in the season of waiting.

Kate is that funny, wise, and honest friend we all want in our lives. So go to your favorite comfy spot, grab a journal and a cup of java. Be prepared to cry, be comforted, and challenged as you make sense of the unexpected single life.

—Jill Monaco
Speaker, relationship coach,
and author of *Freedom Coach Model*

Ghost Ship

For many years now, I have spent my life on the shore, watching, waiting.

Like a million stories told through a hundred generations, I was searching the horizon, looking for someone to come home to me. A companion to walk with. A witness to my life.

I imagined that we would meet on the shore in a glorious homecoming. It would be the moment that all the minutes before had led up to, the moment that in all the minutes after we would never forget.

We would walk hand in hand down the road marked out for us. And when we reached our destination, we would build up our love story around us like a warm shelter.

But years passed. No matter how hard I looked, no matter how fervently I prayed, I did not see that ship coming in. I clenched my cold hands and continued watching on the waterfront, dreaming of the beautiful phantom life that was not mine.

I stood shivering on the shore for a long time, until I realized that the ship, the parallel existence that I had hoped to start living long ago, was a ghost ship. It was perfect, but only because it was elusive. It was beautiful, but only because it was not really there.

I am cold now. I am ready to go somewhere that will hide me from the storm. And so I have a choice—to stay here and watch or to step away from the waiting. Perhaps for a little while, perhaps for the rest of my life. I have a choice to turn my head from the sea and take a slow walk toward a home that I can build for myself right now, today. A decision that will be a beginning and an ending all at once.

The road will be unspeakably beautiful and sometimes painful, just like the journey I would have walked in my parallel life. It will be full of love and full of loneliness, just as it would have been on the sister ship that I never got to ride.

In the end, the path I walk on might not lead me to a home with the arms of a husband or the laughter of children, a reality that may always be difficult for me.

But I can still put flowers in a vase so I can remember small, beautiful things. I can still bake bread and hear laughter around the table. I can still press my face against the windowpane, welcoming the lonely traveler home.

I can wait for that ghost ship forever, or I can build a place where I can rest. A shelter that is heavy with hope, but tempered with acceptance. It will probably never be easy. The longing may never go away. But perhaps God will teach me how to long and let go at the very same time.

One day, someone might knock on my door and sit down with me, warming his hands by the fire I have built. And we may grow to love each other. But if he never comes, my life will still be beautiful, because I have chosen to make it that way.

In the end, I don't want to live in a parallel life that will disappear if I try to touch it. I want to walk out the tangible story that God has set before me today.

Even if I never find the love story that I anticipated, I might find a love story that I didn't expect. A different kind of love story.

A story that leads me home.[1]

Do I Really Need a Minivan in the Game of Life?

I was playing cards with my little friend Isabella the other day. We were playing Old Maid.

You know the game. You each have a set of cards. You draw from the other player and lay down the pairs that you find. Twos, twos, twos. There is anticipation every time a card is drawn from the other player's hand. Who will pair up next?

Another pair, and another pair, and another pair. Each laid down, one right next to the other.

There was one card left in my hand at the end of the game. The old maid. The card had a picture of an older woman surrounded by cats. Apparently cats are the only creatures that will live with single ladies who are mature in age.

Isabella pointed at me and said, "Look, Kate! You have the old maid! That means you're the loser."

I didn't know what to do with this statement or with this game. I don't usually mind losing games to five-year-olds. But I was a little more sensitive about losing this time. In most games, the last person standing wins. In this game, you lose if you're the last person standing alone. I'll let you in on the reason this was difficult for me: I'm thirty-something and I've never been married. I felt a strange kinship with the old maid. "Am I the loser?" I thought.

Old Maid is a very old Victorian game. There are versions around the world, many with different names. In Brazil, it goes by the flattering name Stink. The English version is called Scabby Queen, a name that brings up even worse images than the picture of the American cat lady. And my personal favorite is the French version, Le Pouilleux, which means *the louse*—like the parasitic insect. Another word for louse is cootie. Awesome.

In my research, I also found pictures of some vintage Old Maid games. My favorite was a 1940s deck that had wonderful cartoons of very attractive, curvy women. One woman was riding on an airplane. Another was surfing. A third looked like a successful business lady.

The old maid? A little old lady sitting in a rocking chair knitting, which is quite appropriate, since that is where the word *spinster* comes from. One who spins. It seems that single people who are a little older have nothing better to do than to sit in a rocking chair and knit some booties for their favorite nephew.

A few weeks after this incident, I was playing another game with my ten-year-old friend, Collin. The Game of Life. This game has a track on which players move in little plastic cars through various life scenarios. Interestingly, in the late 1980s the game changed the car from a convertible to a Chrysler-esque minivan.

"Wait a second," I said to Collin. "What if I want a four-wheel drive Subaru instead of a minivan?"

Collin retorted, "You have to have a minivan in the Game of Life."

Well, I realized, it made sense that you would need to have decent leg space in a car, since you have to put your growing family into it.

Your family is acquired toward the beginning of the game, when you hit a stop sign in front of a three-dimensional chapel. It is here that you *must* get married and put a new blue or pink peg beside you in your minivan. I looked at Collin and said, "Hey, what if I don't want to get married? Or what if, by some crazy turn of circumstance, it just doesn't happen for me?"

Collin gave me a quizzical look and said, "You can't do that, Kate! You have to get married in the Game of Life."

It's true. I did. If I didn't, I would be stuck at the beginning of the game. Forever. I gave in, but mostly because you get $5,000 worth of wedding gifts on the next space.

At the end of the game, the bank paid out money for various things. I wasn't at all surprised that you received a decent amount for each child you were able to raise in your minivan. According to Milton Bradley, apparently, he who dies with the most kids gets the most cash.

These are some of the stereotypes that are placed in our minds at a very young age, and I admit I can relate to some of them. Like the old maid, I have seen my friends pair up two-by-two. I am not as old as the old maid in the game, but I am in my thirties, which is pretty old to be single, especially in Christian circles. And yes, I do put my knitted creations on Etsy.

But that's where our similarities stop. I don't like cats, I have many other things to do with my time than to sit in a rocking chair, and I am really, honestly, not a loser.

Those are good signs that I am not really an old maid, right?

There are also things in the Game of Life that I can relate to. I often feel like society says to me, *You're not married? You don't have children? How could you possibly ride around in your plastic car with one lonely plastic peg in it? Is there something wrong? Are you going to get stuck at the beginning of life and never move on to the rest of your game because of your singleness?*

The truth is, I have played a wonderful round of the game of life. I am a songwriter, a worship leader, a writer, and a teacher. I've made several albums and have traveled all over the world to sing my songs and teach. More importantly, I have many dear friends who are like family to me.

Despite this, I get very sad when I look at my car with the one pink peg in it. I never really wanted an empty car. But a family has not been a part of my game yet.

This has been on my mind a lot lately, and after talking about the subject to many friends, I realize that it is on a lot of people's minds. There are more single people in the world than ever before. According to the book *Going Solo*, 22 percent of the adult population was single in the United States in 1950. As of 2012, that statistic has risen drastically to 49 percent.[1]

In other words, there are a lot of us. Some have decided that living independently was the best choice for them. Some are divorced. Others, like me, have always wanted to be married but for some reason have not. All of us have probably struggled with feeling rejected a few times. Maybe many times. We have wanted to feel valuable by being chosen by someone. And most likely, at some point in our lives, we have struggled with feeling like a loser.

I am writing this book for all of you. I want you to feel validated. I want you to know that you're not alone. And most of all, I want you to believe that you are deeply valuable. I hope that we can discover our value together.

Here is what I don't want to do with this book:

I do not want to say that if you follow this formula, you will get yourself a mate. First of all, if I knew that formula, I would already be married. Second, in my experience, God seldom works in formulas.

I do not want to say that the sole answer is to be satisfied in God alone. I believe that it is important to be as deeply connected with the Lord as possible. It is part of the answer. But God loves family, and he understands that our relationship with him is different from a relationship with a flesh and blood person.

I do not want to promise that God will give us the desires of our hearts—at least not in the way that we expect them to be given to us. Ultimately, he will give us our desires, even if it's not in this lifetime.

But the hard truth is that there are people out there who long to be married but never will be. Who want children but won't have any. There are others who will end up with very difficult marriages. We will challenge ourselves to believe in God's goodness even when it seems he is not listening to our prayers.

I do not want to give you the "contentment sermon." We will talk about how important it is to be thankful for where we are in life, but we will also talk about the need to be honest about our feelings. We will look at the paradox of being thankful while still being honest about our frustrations.

Here's what I do want to do with this book:

I want to give hope—and hope for more than a wedding dress.

I want married people and the church at large to have a better understanding of what singles and divorced people go through so that they can better support us.

I want to look at the unique challenges Christian singles face and explore some of the unhealthy perspectives of Christian culture when it comes to dating.

I want to search the beautiful heart of God and discover how he sees us.

I want a wonderful man to read this book, write me romantic love letters, hug dating hello, and marry me, so that my next book will be called *Making Sense of the Scantily Clad Life*.

Our story begins with an event that traditionally ends the story: a wedding. Make that thirty-three weddings.

If You Can't Marry 'Em, Write a Book About 'Em

have been in thirty-three weddings. I am not talking about how many I've been to; I'm talking about how many I've been in.

I'll tell you some of the most memorable.

When I was twenty-two years old, I was a bridesmaid at my friend Andie's wedding. A few years earlier, I set her up with her future husband, Scott. Their wedding was picture-perfect and traditional. Andie wore a beautiful white tulle dress with a long train and veil. Her hair was piled up on her head. Scott wore an all-white tuxedo. The couple sang "If You Could See What I See" into handheld microphones while looking into each other's eyes. The organ played. The wedding vows were exchanged. It was beautiful.

If you watch the VHS tape of their wedding, I am the bridesmaid at the end of the line crying profusely. I'm sure people thought I was crying because it was my best friend getting married and not me. But that was not the reason. I was crying because I was overwhelmed thinking about all the people I loved who were at the wedding. I was thanking God that I had such good friends in my life.

When I was thirty years old, the wedding I was in was the polar opposite of Andie's. It was my brother Will's wedding. The wedding was at a Rainbow Gathering, which is a gathering of about 20,000 people that meet every summer in the national forest. Hippies, Vietnam vets, gutter punks, Hare Krishnas, and everyone in between come together to create a semi-utopian society for about three weeks. I have ministered at the gathering for years, praying for people, leading worship, and giving out food. The believers that I work with every year have become like family to each other.

One year, I invited Will to come to the Rainbow Gathering. He was a shaman at the time. To make an incredible story short, he had a life-changing encounter with God during the gathering that year. He became a follower of Jesus, and he has been one ever since.

Two years later, he married Marie, a dear friend of mine, at the gathering.

I was the wedding coordinator. Marie said to me, "I don't want to do anything. I just want all of our family to give me a wedding." And that's what happened.

Will and Marie got married under a canopy of flowers and branches that our community made for them. There were bagpipes and Irish flutes and about twenty hand drums. The older couples, who loved my brother and his bride like their own children, gathered around Will and Marie and gave them a blessing. Each blessed Will and Marie with the ability to endure something that that particular couple had gone through together, like the ability to make it through a separation, the ability to laugh together, things like that. It was my all-time favorite moment at a wedding.

There was no aisle to walk down at the end of the wedding, so we all circled around the bride and groom and danced. Will spontaneously took Marie's hand and ran with her around a field of sunflowers—God did a fabulous job with the floral design.

Family and friends made the food, baked two cakes, provided the music, made the flower crowns, and did the decorating—all in the middle of the woods. There was something so unique and special about our extended spiritual family coming together to present Will and Marie with their wedding as a gift. It felt like the way a wedding was supposed to be.

Never mind that they spent something like sixty dollars on the wedding. Never mind that I had to walk my shy, conservative dad past mud wrestling in the woods to get there. Never mind that there was a random hippie that walked right up to the couple in the middle of the ceremony to take pictures. It was still the most beautiful wedding I've ever been to.

When I was thirty-two years old, two of my dearest friends and neighbors got married. It was a backyard wedding.

Before it started, I spent some time talking to my friend Shannon. Shannon is one of the spunkiest people I know. She and her husband Daniel have been married twenty years and are still deeply in love. They are big fans of marriage—the friendship, the sex, the overcoming of challenges together, the choosing to love. They talk about these things a lot because they think marriage is such a gift. It's inspiring to see the way they love each other.

This is what Shannon said to me that day, as she gestured toward my curled hair, perfect makeup, and eggplant-colored sleeveless dress that showed off my shoulders: "Kate, you look smoking hot. Too bad it's just wasted."

Most of you singles are probably shaking your heads and putting this comment in the mental file of Insensitive Things Married People Say to Single People.

Believe me, that mental file in my own mind is chock-full of comments people have made to me over the years, but this was not one of them. I was not offended by Shannon's remark because I knew she meant it as a compliment. I actually felt flattered.

I knew that what she was really saying was, "What the heck, Kate? You are beautiful inside and out. I don't understand why you're still single."

People say this to me often. It is kind of a mystery to all of us.

During the wedding, I sang a love song that I had written. At the reception, my married friend Seth said to me, "Kate, in that dress, singing that song, any single guy here would want to dance with you." I was quite flattered.

Thinking about these two comments as I was eating my chicken à la king, I began to feel confident, brazen even. I was beautiful. Someone would want to dance with me.

I started to anticipate the dancing that was about to begin. I imagined one of those handsome, single groomsmen would see me across the room and think, "That was the girl who sang her song during the wedding. She fascinates me. I want to dance with her." He would walk up shyly and ask me. He would gently take my hand and we would step out onto the dance floor together. Even that would give me butterflies, since no one had touched my hand in a long time. And then we would move together. Two people with different personalities, different weaknesses, different strengths, moving as if they were one. Maybe we would even fall in love.

The time came for the single men to ask the single women to dance. I stood at the edge of the floor in anticipation.

No one asked me to dance.

I wanted to say, "Hey! Single guys! Over here! According to my married friends, this dress makes me look smoking hot! Doesn't anyone want to dance with me?"

I hoped the next song would be falling-in-love worthy.

The next song was anything but romantic. It had nothing to do with wedded bliss and everything to do with an athletic club.

That's right, folks: "YMCA."

Up until that day, I never understood why this song was a staple at wedding receptions. I stood on the dance floor pondering this phenomenon.

Hmmm, I thought. *The Hokey Pokey was probably invented so that wallflowers who never learned how to jitterbug could go out there and shake their booties. It gave them permission. It was part of the song: "You put your backside in, you put your backside out."*

"YMCA" became the Hokey Pokey of the 80s. If you hadn't learned the incredibly complicated 80s dance that involved hopping up and down, you could at least fling your arms out to spell things.

Look at us! Who says we can't dance? We are so coordinated! We can all spell out the acronym of the Young Men's Christian Association in perfect unison!

Finally, I gathered up my gumption and danced with all the other bad dancers. More accurately, I spelled. If you looked closely, though, you would realize that I wasn't in perfect unison with everyone else, because instead of spelling YMCA, I was spelling WPCD. A secret joke between me and myself: White People Can't Dance. This has been a tradition for me at weddings ever since.

The next song was the Macarena, which was the Hokey Pokey of the 90s. This song has the same concept: a dance that even a person in a wheelchair could do. Again, what does this dance have to do with the sealing of a covenant between two people?

In the songs that followed, I participated in all of the traditional dances performed at Caucasian-majority weddings. You know, like the squat, the double-squat-spin-clap-and-point, the clap-point-point-clap-point-point-and-squat, the hip-breaker, the Caucasian-clap, the point-to-the-Lord, and the fat-rebel.

Finally, toward the end of the reception, the DJ put on the music I really wanted to dance to, even if it was reminiscent of awkward middle school moments.

But no one asked me. There would be no slow dancing for me. Not even in my smoking hot dress.

I wanted love, and, instead, I got the white man's overbite. Seriously, God? Seriously?

That night was like a snapshot of my life. At the beginning of the reception, I sat at the table with good friends and ate. I laughed. I loved being in their company. I was thankful.

But then the dancing came and everyone took his partner to dance. Another pair and another pair and another pair. Twos, twos,

twos. I sat at the table and slowly ate my wedding cake, an important activity when you don't want to look like you have nothing to do while everyone else is dancing. I cried in the bathroom stall.

This time, it really was because it was not my wedding.

I don't want my singleness to be hard for me. I want to be satisfied in who I am as a single woman. But when I look at those pairs dancing, no matter how hard I try to fight it, I don't feel smoking hot. I feel alone.

I try to remember that I have a wonderful life, as single lives go. I also try to realize that I have it better than almost any single older woman in any other moment in history had it. If I lived as a single woman in another country or in another time, I would be less worried about being a loser and more worried about being alive. I am blessed to live in a time in which I can work to take care of myself and in which I don't need a husband to survive. I try to appreciate my freedom and independence as a single woman.

And yet, if it were my choice, I believe I would give up some of my independence to understand what it's like to be in covenant with someone, even if it were difficult. To have people in my life who were more than just my spiritual family, but who were my blood family. To have a husband and children who would walk with me on this journey. I know that marriage is not the fairy tale our culture makes it out to be, but I still want it.

I never expected to be single at this age. I thought I would have a family by now. I have had to rearrange my life accordingly, and that has been very difficult for me.

In the preface I talked about the *ghost ship,* the parallel life that I sometimes feel I am missing out on. A life in which I have a family.

Part of the problem is that I don't know what that parallel life would really look like. Right now it is just a mystery, a fairy tale. If I were actually in that parallel life, I would probably have days in which I felt useless. I would be exhausted from taking care of my kids. I would most likely feel like the romance between my husband

and me waned at times, which would be difficult. I would have relational challenges I can't even begin to imagine right now. These are the things that my married friends struggle with every day.

My view of the life of my married friends is probably not realistic, in the same way that their view of my life can be romanticized. All that freedom! All that traveling! I do have a lot of freedom, but that's because the nature of covenant is that lines are drawn around the people within it. I have a lot of freedom because I don't have a lot of covenant. I often struggle with feeling like my life means less because I have no children and no family to invest in.

All the while, my married friends could be sitting at home in their own day-to-day lives, wondering if their lives mean anything because they are at home every day, trying to understand how to connect to the people they love. Many of them, I'm sure, are wondering about their own parallel lives—lives that do not involve marriage or children.

As my friend Aaron said to me the other day, "We spend the first half of our lives trying to meet the one we will marry. We spend the second half of our lives trying to connect with that person."

Most of us, single or married, struggle with the same root sadness of feeling lonely. One of our biggest fears is to be alone. A 2005 Gallup poll about what people fear the most revealed terrorist attacks, death, nuclear war, and, you guessed it, being alone.[1] All of us struggle with it.

I recently heard an interview with David Blaine, the world-famous illusionist and endurance artist. Blaine has lived in a coffin for seven days where he ate and drank nothing but a few tablespoons of water per day. He has been encased in ice for sixty-three hours. He has stood on a hundred-foot-high pillar for thirty-five hours. He has held his breath for over seventeen minutes on the Oprah Winfrey show, beating a world record at the time. He lived in a Plexiglas box suspended over the Thames river for forty-four days, again on only a little water a day.

It could be argued that this is the least fearful human being on the planet. But the interviewer asks Blaine, "Is there anything that you're afraid of?" Without hesitating, he replies, "No." Then he pauses for a second. "You know, I could say one thing now that I think about it, though. If I have to go sleep in like a big house somewhere and no one else is there, I can't do it. I'd rather just sleep on the street."[2]

This makes me feel better. I may not be able to hold my breath for seventeen minutes, but I have slept in a big empty bed for over thirty years. So you see, even the bravest soul on earth is frightened of being alone.

All of us desire three basic things: to be loved for who we are, to feel like we're valuable, and to know we're not alone. For some mysterious reason, we have a really hard time knowing how to give and receive those things.

And yet we want them. We yearn for them. More than wealth. More than success. More than anything. We want to be seen, understood, and loved. Loved in our strong places; loved in our weak places.

Known.

Where did this desire come from? Is a life that has no intimate witness still known? If we never become part of a traditional family, are we doomed to loneliness or can we build our own, different family? What do we do when no one asks us to dance? Does God see me alone at my table, eating my wedding cake? Does he care? Does he ever feel the same way? These are some of the questions we will explore in the chapters to come.

Kate: The Musical

I am sitting in my backyard in Colorado during the changing of the light, my favorite time of day. I have a laptop perched on my knees and a cup of tea beside me.

And my mind is on you.

I am thinking about the fact that out of all the words in the world, you have chosen to read mine. I am honored that you would do that, and I want to welcome you into my story as best I can.

It is tempting to simply give you advice, to tell you about awkward dating moments, or to explore a passage of scripture about God's view on singleness. It would be less vulnerable to only take these angles and leave out anything personal about my life.

But I want to do more than that in this book. I want you to understand that we are really not that different at all.

So, for now, pretend that you are sitting in the lawn chair next to me, looking toward the Flatirons rock formations in Boulder, Colorado, sipping chamomile. I am telling you about the journey I have walked to get where I am tonight. A path that has brought me places I did not expect. A path that has been full of frustration and questioning, but a path that has also been full of joy and great love.

In that way, it is probably a story very much like yours.

I will start by saying that I want to honor my family while I write, so I won't get into too many details about my childhood. It is enough to tell you that I was a sad little girl, and that I had good reasons to be sad. I had to grow up very fast. I can safely say that my first fifteen years were some of the most difficult of my life.

I am a songwriter. My songs often bring glimpses of my journey, so I am going to write out certain lyrics for you throughout this chapter when I feel like that song best expresses what I am trying to say.

I wrote a song years ago contemplating what it would be like to go back to the little girl that I used to be and to have a conversation with her. I would tell her that she is trying so hard. That she is so strong. But she would have a hard time believing those things. She doesn't see herself as strong or beautiful. She sees herself as the short-haired girl with funny thrift store clothes who people think is a boy. She sees herself as the one without any friends. She sees herself as a girl who will most likely turn into a woman who will fall into divorce and abuse and all the things that are part of her life now.

I would hold her in my arms and tell her how brave she is. I would tell her that she can't even imagine all of the beautiful moments awaiting her. That someday, she will travel the world and be amazed by it. That she will have family and friends who deeply love her, something I know she prays for every day. And most of all, I would tell her that she will someday know the unconditional love of her Creator, who already loves her deeply, and that his love will change everything for her.

These are the words of the song that I wrote for that little girl:

> I see a little girl in the back of my mind
> See daisies in her hand,
> She's looking to the sky, she is looking to the sky.
> She is sitting on the stairs of her two-story house
>   and the pain that she bears
> Leaves no tears left to cry, leaves her no tears left to cry.
> Where is the reward for the ones who have been torn?

Where is the treasure laid for the ones who've known so
    much pain?
Hey little girl let me whisper some hope.
There's mercy for you that overflows.
Everything's going to be all right
Everything's going to be all right.
Hey little girl won't you hear me say
There is love enough to cover your shame.
Everything's going to be all right
Everything's going to be all right.
And that little girl so small and so scared
Has been near so long I forgot she was there,
I forgot that she was there.
Somehow the pain that she didn't feel passed on to me
A weight too great to bear
Much too great to bear.
Someone is standing near
Who will wash away her tears.
Someday when she's been found
Her scars will become a crown.[1]

After these difficult years as a young girl and an adolescent, I
went to high school. It was there that I met some wonderful believing friends who took me in. I started following Jesus. It was the first
time I felt like part of a family. Those were very happy years.

Then I entered college. It's the only time in your life where you
constantly get to consume semi-edible all-you-can-eat-food and live
in a small town filled with people your own age, a town in which
most people's careers involve finding their identity by getting totally
wasted. I knew from high school that you don't really need to get
drunk to have ridiculous amounts of fun. You just need to play
Chubby Bunny. So that's what I did.

About halfway through my freshman year, I dated my first serious boyfriend. It was wonderful and romantic at first, but soon

dating him triggered a deep place of wounding in me and sent me into a serious depression.

Those of you who have been depressed understand when I say I was drowning in my sadness. I knew that Kate—the Kate that I liked and other people liked—was deep in there somewhere. But I couldn't find her. It was as if she was trapped in a fathomless dark well and she had no clue how to climb out of it.

Up to this point, I mostly had been a Christian for the benefits of Christianity. I had family all around me. I got to date guys who didn't call me mean names. If I said the right thing in Sunday school, people would think I was valuable.

Now, all of that was stripped away. My boyfriend broke up with me, saying I was not the same person he had started dating nine months before. People who admired me as a strong believer wondered what was wrong with me and where my faith had gone. Even my dear friends who tried hard to be there for me told me they didn't know how to help me and I was going to need professional help.

All I had left was God. And I didn't know if he was going to be enough.

I was so overwhelmed with grief at times that all I could do was to go back in the woods behind my apartment and cry out to this God who I couldn't seem to reach. Sometimes I would spend six hours there, crying.

After about a year of this depression, I went on a mission trip in Mexico. There was a little cove next to the ocean where I went when I needed time to cry.

One day, as I lay huddled and weeping by the beach, I said, "Lord, at this point, I don't think I can have a family, a job, a life. I am too sad. I feel like I am going crazy. Are you ever going to make me better?"

As clearly as I have ever heard God speak to me, he said, "Kate, look at the ocean." I looked at it, crashing back and forth and back and forth like it has since the beginning of time. "As many times as the ocean waves keep crashing back to the shore, that's how many times I'm going to heal you. That's how many times I'm going to restore you. That's how many times I'm going to wash you clean."

Up to that point, I had been hearing a lot of lies in my head and I was believing them. Things like, "You aren't worth anything," "No one loves you," and "You will never be happy."

But when I heard that promise from God about the ocean that night, I believed him.

I started dancing around the beach, singing and crying. My heart was full of joy for the first time in a long time.

That night was a turning point of that season and, subsequently, of my entire life. I understood that the God who created me also cared about every detail of my life.

I had what all humans long for. I was loved.

My song "You Are Not Alone" is my reflection on this deep truth that changed my life.

> Sometimes you get so weary that you run to forget
> You keep yourself so busy anything to cover up that
> Sometimes life just don't make sense
> And the reason for your running is a longing to be
>   known
> By someone who says your life is worth it, someone
>   captured by your heart
> Someone you gave up on long ago
> But you are not alone
> You are not alone
> His love is all around
> He holds you even now
> You are not alone
> He will not leave you orphaned, that's a promise he has
>   made
> When others leave you empty and the world has left
>   you broken

Still he will not walk away
So come and lay down all your questions
Lay down your striving to be free
He has loved you since you've breathed and
He will love you for forever
Really what more do you need?[2]

The four years that followed my college years run together in a
blur. They were restless years. I worked at a daycare on and off. I
wrote songs that I never sang for anyone. The words *God, please show
me what I'm supposed to do* were written over and over again in my
journal. This made sense, because these were my "supposed to" years.
I wanted God to hand things to me with a perfect bow on them so
I wouldn't have to make decisions.

I dated someone seriously during that season, but I was unsure
if I wanted to marry him. I distinctly remember him saying, "Kate,
I don't want you to just ask God if you're supposed to marry me. I
want you to also ask yourself if you want to marry me."

I didn't like that question because I didn't know what I wanted.
A year later, we broke up. I was devastated.

Soon after that, I moved to Colorado Springs to work with Ben
and Robin Pasley, the musicians who started the Enter the Worship
Circle series, which are acoustic, organic, live, and life-changing
albums. I had the privilege of writing and singing on one of the
albums in the series. Ben and Robin mentored me for the next few
years, teaching me how to use my music as a means to love people
and share the gospel. I developed my mission statement, which was
(and is) "to paint an accurate picture of a passionate God."

For the next ten years I traveled as a music missionary. It would
take up a whole book to tell you all the adventures I have had while
touring. I have led worship at hippie gatherings where a naked guy
spat on the cross and a woman wearing fur stood in front of me yelling, "Praise Mother Earth!" I have sung Christian hard rock songs
in which I was required to head bang in front of two thousand

people in Thailand. I have played in castles in Germany. I have taught homeless people about music and recorded an album of their songs. I have played shows where it was just me and five other people. I have taught students who rose up to become a new generation of worship leaders in Southern Ireland. I have sung spontaneous love songs from God over women in rehab recovering from heroin addictions, watching them weep one by one.

It has been a full, incredible ten years.

I had a handful of boyfriends and serious crushes during this season. You will get an idea about these relationships as you read this book, but they were all similar. They basically looked like this: Boy meets girl. Girl really really really likes boy. Boy is pretty sure he likes girl. Girl is very in love but afraid of being abandoned. Boy thinks girl is amazing and cares about her but is unsure if she is "the one." Boy breaks up with girl. Girl is in the depths of despair.

Lather, rinse, repeat.

Somewhere in the middle of this, I was bitten by a tick while ministering in Michigan. I went to the doctor to get tested for Lyme disease, and it came back negative.

For the next ten years, I had all kinds of bizarre health problems. I almost lost my finger to gangrene. I had arthritis all over my body. Huge welts showed up on my skin. I would spit blood. When I was at my worst, I lost 35 pounds in two months.

And then there was the insomnia. I barely slept through the night. I could go seven, eight days without sleeping day or night. When I did sleep, it was only for about three hours or so, and then I would wait nights before I got another three hours. I often had panic attacks when I would try to sleep. This went on for years. My best friend told me years later that when I would leave her house after lying on her couch all day so I wouldn't have to be alone, she would cry because she thought I might not live very long.

I finally went to a doctor who said that every specialist I had seen before and every test had been wrong. I did, indeed, have Lyme disease.

I believed that God heals. I had seen him do it many times. Why wasn't he listening to my prayers for my own healing? I was being tortured by my lack of sleep. I was in pain all the time and I wanted to be in hot water every second of the day. I was completely exhausted. I felt like I was going crazy.

Where was the God who had been so faithful to me in the past?

As I was lying in bed night after night, begging God for sleep, having absolutely no idea why the God who loved me would not heal me, I would talk to my soul. I would say, "Soul, this does not make sense right now. But you cannot, you CANNOT let go of believing in God's goodness."

One of my favorite passages of scripture, which I memorized during my depression in college, is Psalm 30. It says:

> Weeping may stay for the night,
>   but rejoicing comes in the morning...
> You turned my wailing into dancing;
>   you removed my sackcloth and clothed me with joy,
>   that my heart may sing your praises and not be silent.
> Lord my God, I will praise you forever
> (Psalm 30:5,11-12).

One morning, when my health was at its worst, when I had no strength to get out of bed, I rolled over to my keyboard. I laid my head down on it because I could not keep it up. I put my fingers on the keys and started playing. God gave me a song based out of Psalm 30, a song to sing to my own soul.

Often I write songs for the people who will listen. But this song was for me, to give me hope. It's called, "Joy Comes in the Morning."

> Awake oh my soul wipe the sleep from your eyes
> Look and see what you missed before
> Do not give up hope though you've wept through the
>   night

Your light will break forth like the dawn
Joy comes in the morning
Joy comes in the morning
Joy comes in the morning
Why are you downcast,
Put your hope in the Lord
He makes all things beautiful
Remember how he's rescued you before
Be strong now lift your head
Joy comes in the morning
Joy comes in the morning
Joy comes in the morning.[3]

I tried hard to believe the words to that song were true.

This was one of the most difficult seasons of my life to be single. I wanted a companion with me, someone who could care about finding a way for me to get better simply so that I could rest. Someone who could hold me at night and tell me it was going to be okay. I wondered if I could ever have that, if anyone would ever love me enough to take on such a huge burden.

I remember coming home from a doctor's appointment during which the doctor had let me know how serious my disease was. He told me that I could pass it on to my children. There was a slight chance I could give it to my husband if I didn't get better. I wondered if I should just opt out of having a family then and there. I didn't want my husband or children to have to live through this. The doctor also told me that with Lyme, my symptoms would probably get worse for the rest of my life, that it would be almost impossible to cure it.

I stood in my living room after that appointment, my purse and coat still on, and I suddenly became overwhelmed with the weight of responsibility on my shoulders. I was the only one in my life who could get help for this. I was so sick that I could barely walk into a grocery store, yet I was expected to do the hard work of living day to day with such a debilitating disease. I had no insurance and probably could not get insurance with the record I now had. I couldn't work, and the government would not give me disability as Lyme is not a very recognized disease.

I was terrified, and I was alone.

The Alcoholics Anonymous Big Book says, "When we were faced with a crisis that we could no longer postpone or evade we had to fearlessly face the proposition that either God is everything or else he is nothing. Choose."[4]

It was time for me to choose. Was God everything or nothing to me?

That night I had a dream. I was riding up an elevator and the doors opened. I was in a hospital. A middle-aged man, slightly overweight and with the kindest face I had ever seen, came up and gave me a big bear hug. I had the distinct impression that we had started out as pen pals, and over the years we had become very close. He was so happy to see me.

I said, "How is she doing?"

He replied, "She is not well." He had so much concern in his face. I could tell that he loved her with a very pure love.

It was then that I realized that the "she" we were talking about was me. The sick version of me. Suddenly, I was the sick me, in my hospital bed. I was in and out of a coma, and I was very, very sick.

Every single time I woke up, this man was there. Reading to me, doing crossword puzzles, holding my hand. Sometimes I would wake up and he would be eating in the room. He never left my side. Most of the time, I was too sick to say anything. I would just look and see him there and know that I wasn't alone. Then I would fall back into another coma.

Sometimes, he would pick me up and put me into my wheelchair. There was a huge outdoor garden on my floor in the hospital, and he would bring me to look at all the beautiful plants and flowers. He would touch them tenderly and tell me their names and about how they grew. He would take my weak hands and bring them up to the flowers. I could feel the petals on my fingers.

He would take me back to my room, lift me out of my wheelchair and into my bed, and I would fall back to sleep as he knelt there, praying.

When I woke up from the dream I realized that the man was not a future husband or a father or a friend. It was Jesus.

Our God has many facets. Sometimes he is riding on a horse with stars in his right hand and a sword coming from his mouth, his face shining like the sun. Sometimes, he is a middle-aged, kind man who reads to us when we are in the hospital. He is the one who kneels down and prays for us by our sick bed. He is the one who does not leave our side.

This dream helped me remember that I was everything to him, and that made my choice simple: He would be everything to me.

Soon after this, God led me to a brilliant naturopathic doctor named Dr. Shauna Young, whom I now credit with saving my life, or at least with saving me from a very difficult life of chronic illness.[5]

I was officially declared free of Lyme disease in June 2009, seven years to the day after I was bitten by the tick. I have absolutely no arthritis anymore, no pain. I have energy. Most nights, I am finally sleeping through the night, now that my brain has had a few years to heal.

I try to thank God every day for my health now.

In the years that followed my getting better, I went through another depression following a breakup with my boyfriend of two and a half years. I have mourned getting older and not having a family. But one thing I have learned through my journey is this:

God has rescued me before. He will rescue me again.

I am in a mostly happy season right now. I am healthy. I have the most beautiful community surrounding me to walk through life with. I am doing what I love. I still want a family very much, but I am learning day by day to trust God with my desires.

Song of Songs 8:5 says, "Who is this coming up from the wilderness, leaning on her beloved?" That verse perfectly describes the journey that I am on now. I am coming up out of the wilderness leaning on my beloved. There are a lot of things I don't understand, especially being single. But I do know that I can lean on Jesus. I know that he is trustworthy. And I know that I will never walk alone, no matter what wilderness or mountaintops await me.

The Rant Chapter

I have tried to live with everything in balance. Favoring one side of the scale all the time will bring chaos. Yin and yang—the harmony of things—is a healthy way to live.

Yin Yin—the imbalance of things—is not a healthy way to live. But it would make a great name for a panda bear.

I promise to bring balance soon. I will discuss in later chapters the wisdom of having realistic expectations of marriage, of being thankful, of looking to God for solace and stability and comfort. You know, all of the things you expect to hear in a book about being single.

But first I need to validate all the singles reading this book. I think we all need to feel understood, even if just for a little while. I will attempt to sound wise and wonderful for most of this book. But during this one itsy-bitsy chapter, I am asking your permission to sound a little bitter and mean. If you don't like ranting, skip to the next chapter.

Because at the risk of sounding like I am ranting, I am going to rant.

Here goes. Let these words resonate in all of their pity-party glory. Let this sentence be as naked as I want to be someday.

Being single sucks.

There it is, folks. The sentiment almost every single person has thought many, many times—especially those of us who are over thirty. For decades, it has not been socially acceptable in the Christian world to articulate that sentiment without feeling like children throwing a temper tantrum about our love lives.

And I just said it. I should get a Dove award or something.

I know that sentence makes me sound unspiritual, ungrateful, and untrusting. In fact, I have been thinking about rewriting it many times since I typed it.

I read a good book this week, one that I wouldn't have had time for if I had a family, so I pondered changing the sentence to "Sometimes being single sucks."

I babysat five kids today, and I was as frazzled as a one-legged Riverdancer. I thought about adding, "but having a family is difficult too."

Finally, though, I decided to leave it like it is. Nothing softening the blow, nothing added to the end of the sentence. Why?

Because someone needs to say it. That's why.

Something seems to have thrown me over the edge. Maybe it's the website I was on this morning. When suggesting a password question, it gave me, "The date you and your spouse met" or, "The maid of honor in your wedding" or, "Your first child's birthday." I inevitably had to choose, "The name of your first cat." Even if Samone was the best cat in the world, she was still a friggin' cat.

Maybe it's that when I see a couple kiss, even just in passing, it makes my heart ache a little bit. It makes me think that if I were ever to have that again, I would try to appreciate even the briefest moment of us expressing that we have chosen each other, that we are closer to each other than we are to anyone else in the world.

Maybe it's that I have no idea what to put on my phone's screen saver. I guess a mountain or something.

Maybe it's that I spend about seventy percent of an average day alone. I have spent years like this. Sometimes, it can get unbearably lonely.

Maybe it's that I often feel like I have been perpetually living the life of a college student, roommates and all, for the last fifteen years. I don't even want to think about how many times I've moved during that time.

Maybe it's that I often avoid spending time with my friends' children because I end up wanting to cry almost the entire time.

Maybe it's the story I heard recently about my friend's Bible study, during which an older single woman started crying and talking about her struggles with feeling lonely. A married member of the group scoffed, "Why don't you take my kids for a day and I'll go get my nails done?"

Maybe it's that I really hate small talk and I really hate getting my hopes up and I really hate hurting people, so I would rather have my teeth drilled than go on eHarmony first dates. I know, I know, all you married people! Online dating is the ultimate answer to my singleness woes! I know that there are a hundred men waiting for me in the online dating world! But ninety-nine of those men are showing off their beer bellies with their shirts off (I'm serious, I've had that match), or they have a profile picture with their arm around their ex-girlfriends, or most commonly, they don't love God like I do. I have to go through a lot of awkwardness and pain to possibly, maybe, find the one out of the ninety-nine. I know that sometimes you need to have a root canal to get a new tooth, so I'm giving it a try. But that doesn't mean I have to like it.

Maybe it's that while doing research for this book, I found countless articles with titles like, "Marriage Does Not Solve Your Problems," or "How to Stop Postponing Your Life," but none called something like, "Why Singleness Sucks."

Take this quotation, for example, from one of the above articles: "Marriage is about finding a comrade, not ultimate contentment. It's about finding a helpmate, not a healer."[1] I read countless sentiments like this in my research. Here's the thing: I don't think that I have postponed my life. I have tried to live life fully with the hand I have been given. And I am not looking for ultimate contentment or for a healer. I know that contentment is something that I have to work out between myself and God and that I shouldn't project it onto another person. I already have a healer, and I realize that. But I am longing for a comrade, a lifelong companion, a helpmate, and it hurts that I don't have one yet. Is there something wrong with that? Are my feelings not valid?

One of the only articles I found that did talk about the difficulty of being single was called "My Secret Grief: Over Thirty-Five, Single, and Childless" by Melanie Notkin. In it, the author says, "This type of grief, grief that is not accepted or that is silent, is referred to as *disenfranchised grief*. It's the grief you don't feel allowed to mourn, because your loss isn't clear or understood. You didn't lose a sibling or a spouse or a parent. But losses that others don't recognize can be as powerful as the kind that is socially acceptable."[2]

This article put into words something I have experienced for years but have never been able to put a finger on. It's the idea of disenfranchised grief. Disenfranchised means to deprive someone of their legal right. Therefore, disenfranchised grief means to deprive someone of their right to grieve.

Our culture has unknowingly taught us that we are grieving in the wrong way or that we have no right to grieve at all.

When my dad died, I lost something tangible. People called me. They held me when I cried and asked me to talk about what I was going through. They came to his memorial service. It meant the world to me. I needed family around me during that grieving process. People bound up the wounds, told me it was going to be okay, and walked with me through the healing process. They rose to the occasion and helped me recover.

When it comes to being in my thirties and facing the prospect of not having a traditional family, though, people don't know what to do with my frustration. "There's nothing there. How could you be in pain?"

The truth is, I am in pain precisely because there is nothing there. The loss is over something that never existed, and that is what makes it so elusive. I have never lost a child but I have never had a child. I've never lost a husband but I've never had a lover.

The truth is, the loss of something that did exist and the mourning over something that never existed are both very, very difficult. Unintentionally and silently, we are told that there is no reason to grieve over our singleness. And so we are sometimes deprived of our right to grieve.

This is a different kind of bereavement because it is painful in a slow, seeping kind of way. It's a dull loss of which I am reminded many times a day. Each reminder aches a little bit and adds to the larger ache inside of me. Every day I have to consciously choose to find joy despite these reminders, and that choice can be exhausting.

There are funny ways that church culture reflects most people's unawareness of our disenfranchised loss—not in what they do give us, but in what they don't give us. The sermons that aren't given, the prayers that aren't offered, the books that aren't written. As if what we are going through is not that important.

I remember going to a church service where a pastor tearfully prayed for people in different predicaments: "Lord, I pray for the married people who are struggling through the difficulties of relationship right now. For the divorced people who are wrestling with rejection. And for the single people who (cue a bit of chuckling) don't know how good they have it."

Pastors are almost never single, so they don't often teach on singleness. It is not the particular struggle they are going through, so they often overlook it. I have heard people say that it wouldn't be fair for a pastor to preach on singleness because so many of the members of the congregation wouldn't be able to relate. But factoring in students, older singles, the divorced, and the widowed, most churches likely have a large portion of their congregation that is single. We singles have listened to countless sermons on marriage. We have often tried to learn from sermons about family and marriage, even though we can't completely relate to them. It would be nice to have married people give us the same consideration at times.

Similarly, there are thousands of books, even just in the Christian genre, about marriage. But there are only a handful about being single. And the ones about singleness are often about getting a mate, maintaining purity, or being content with the gift of singleness.

I mentioned this to a well-meaning married friend the other day, and she said, "Of course there are thousands of books on marriage! It just shows you how difficult it is to be married. All of those books on marriage are needed since it's so hard."

The "marriage is so hard" speech is one of the most popular speeches given to single people, right up there with the "if you just let go" speech, which I will discuss later.

I wanted to say to my friend, "Oh yes, it's a breeze to wake up every morning wondering if you will ever be chosen, if you will ever be intimate with anyone, if you will ever have children. These are things that even people in the Bible mourned over! It's really quite easy to think that I might not ever have anyone call me *Mom*. That if I don't get married I will always wonder where to go for Christmas because I don't have my own husband and kids to celebrate with. I have no qualms with the haunting thought that if I am still single as an older woman, I will not have a husband or children to take care of me, or even to talk to. That's all really easy. No wonder there are so few books out there about it."

Okay. I think I am mostly done now. Thank you for letting me rant; it felt really good. I will talk in my "nice Kate" voice again.

Let me emphasize that I didn't just go on that rant for the sake of being angry. I simply wanted to take the opportunity to say that singles want so much to be seen.

There have certainly been occasions when teachers have validated singles, and their words felt like water to my soul. I remember the time that one of my spiritual papas, Chuck Parry, had all the couples in church stand in a circle. Then, he had the single men stand in a circle inside the larger circle. Then, he had the single women stand inside of the men's circle. He said, "This is the kind of family we need to be. We need to remember and protect our daughters." That meant the world to me.

Last week I went to a conference hosted by InnerChange, an organization that sends teams of missionaries to move into poor neighborhoods around the world in order to bring the gospel. The conference featured a panel to discuss the topic of families, and, shockingly, there were several single people on the panel. The panel spent the majority of the time talking about the single people on their teams and how the other team members could bless these singles and be family to them, since the singles didn't have a traditional family of their own. The panel discussed how married people should never reduce singles to live-in babysitters. They talked about how the singles should be able to speak into the lives of the married people on the team, that they should never be considered lower on the totem pole because of their relationship status, and that singles should be able to be leaders over the married people if that was the best fit.

The couples asked the single people on the panel how the married people on their teams could benefit them and help them through the challenges of being single. I was so honored that they noticed people like me, that they remembered us, and that they validated our relational challenges, even if we don't have spouses and children to deal with. They considered our voices important when talking about families, a discussion we were usually left out of.

I had to nonchalantly wipe my mascara-trailed cheeks and runny nose with a page from my journal. I was so touched that someone would remember me in my singleness and address issues that I always thought I had to hide. I would love to see the church rise up to bring more validation to the singles in their own congregations in similar ways.

Though there have been occasions like the last two examples that have made me feel validated as a single person, most of the time my disenfranchised grief is overlooked in the church. I don't get a lot of good support or information that helps me cope with being thirty-something and single.

It helps me to remember that even when no one around me understands my pain, God understands. He doesn't want me to dwell in it or drown in it, but he does want to meet me where I am and let me know that he understands.

One of the stories that has ministered the most to me in this season of being single is the story of Hannah, the mother of Samuel. She was one of two wives of a man named Elkanah. Elkanah's other wife was named Peninnah. Peninnah had many children, but Hannah was barren.

Elkanah mourned with her that she couldn't have children. Peninnah was cruel to Hannah, however, and would mock her for not having any children. You can imagine what she might have said to Hannah: "Where is your God now? He seems to have blessed me and kept you barren. I wonder why that's happening to you. Maybe you did something wrong? Maybe you're not good enough?"

Does that sound familiar?

Hannah would weep bitterly and mourn so much that she wouldn't be able to eat anything.

Her husband would come to her and say, "Hannah, why are you weeping? Why don't you eat? Why are you downhearted? Don't I mean more to you than ten sons?" Though she knew that her husband loved her, she still mourned over what she did not have. She longed for a child.

She went to the temple and made a vow to the Lord. She said, "O Lord Almighty, if you will only look upon your servant's misery, and remember me, and not forget your servant but give her a son, then I will give him to the Lord for all the days of his life."

The priest, Eli, saw Hannah in all of her passion. He was not used to seeing someone worship in such an emotional way, so he assumed she was drunk.

He admonished her, but she said, "I am a woman who is deeply troubled. I have not been drinking. I was pouring out my soul to the LORD. Do not take your servant for a wicked woman; I have been praying here out of my great anguish and grief."

Eli said, "Go in peace, and may the God of Israel grant you what you have asked of him" (1 Samuel 1:1-18).

"Then she went and ate something, and her face was no longer downcast." Notice here that even before her prayer was answered, she lifted her head. The simple act of pouring out her heart to God gave her hope.

The next day, she woke up and worshipped with her husband. And then they went home.

In the course of time, God joyfully answered Hannah's prayer. She conceived and bore a son and named him Samuel. Samuel means "God heard me."

When her son was born, she worshipped God with this beautiful prayer:

> My heart rejoices in the LORD;
> in the LORD is my horn lifted high.
> My mouth boasts over my enemies,
> for I delight in your deliverance.
> There is no one holy like the LORD;
> there is no one besides you;
> there is no Rock like our God...
> for the LORD is a God who knows...
> He raises the poor from the dust
> and lifts the needy from the ash heap;
> he seats them with princes
> and has them inherit a throne of honor
> (1 Samuel 2:1-3,8).

In some ways, her prayer was more than worship. It was prophecy.

When Hannah prayed this prayer, her nation had no king; judges were the leaders of Israel in that era. She was, perhaps, foreseeing that this son that God gave her would do great things, including anointing the first two kings of Israel, Saul and David, ushering them into their reign.

In the next few years Hannah conceived three more sons and two daughters, but she kept her promise to God with her first son. Samuel grew up in the temple. Samuel was born as a result of his mother's worship, so it made sense that he would be raised in a place of worship.

Samuel was raised by Eli, the priest. Eli had two sons who were also priests, but they were evil. Samuel, however, heard and followed God's voice from a very young age. In a long line of corrupt leaders, he grew up to be a political leader who ruled by listening to God.

Samuel was the bridge of the old era to a new era. He was considered the last judge of Israel and the first prophet of Israel. The political atmosphere of the country completely changed with Samuel. It went from a place where leaders made decisions by judging to a place where leaders listened and responded to God. Just as God did not judge Hannah but listened to her, Samuel was able to access a God who not only judged, but who also listened.

A nation was changed forever, and it all came from a hurting woman who didn't hide her disappointment from God but who poured it out to him instead.[3]

Do you know what I love most about this story? I love that Hannah let herself mourn. I love that she used words like "great anguish and grief," "misery," and "deeply troubled." Have you felt pain that deep before? I know that I have. Have you been like me, trying to cover up how raw and real those emotions are? Avoiding words that describe how much you ache? Hiding your pain from God because you fear that you would seem ungrateful if you questioned why life doesn't make sense?

About eight years ago, I bought a dining room table from a thrift store for my birthday. The table was very dusty, but when I rubbed off some of the dust, I saw how beautiful it was. It was made of dark wood, with claw and ball legs and chairs with flowers etched into them. I don't often spend money on myself; I felt foolish even wanting the table. But in my mind's eye, as clear as day as I stood in that thrift store, I saw myself sitting with a family around that table. I saw us talking about our days. I saw friends having deep conversations with us over dinner. I saw children running around, playing hide-and-go-seek, laughing.

I bought that table as a gift of hope to myself. I had a great expectation that those things would happen around that very table.

After many years of use my brother and sister-in-law kept the table since I was traveling and not in a stable home for a season. After a while, they decided to move away, and I couldn't afford to come get the table. They wanted to sell it. I kicked and screamed. I did not want to sell that table. I thought maybe my older brother would take it, but he didn't. There wasn't room for the table in my new house. I knew that I had to let it go.

The table was worth some money, but it wasn't in the best shape. I put ads up, asking for eight hundred dollars. I talked about how priceless the table was, how beautiful. No one budged. Down to five hundred. And down and down and down.

Finally, my brother sold it at a garage sale for two hundred dollars.

It was more than a table to me. It was attached to my dreams. Nearly a decade after buying the table, those dreams had not come to pass. They were sold at a garage sale for a couple hundred bucks.

I believe that when that table was sold, God did for me what he did for Hannah. He did not mock my sadness over a piece of furniture. He knew it was not a little thing to me. He knew that I was disappointed, and he let me mourn.

God did not say to Hannah (like her husband, Elkanah, said), "You are so ungrateful! You have a husband who loves you. Isn't that enough?" Nor did he say, "Be still, my child. Know that I am God. I, and only I, can fill this empty place in you."

No, God did not answer her that way. He heard her prayer. He heard the cry of her heart and he understood. He listened. And I believe he ached with her, just as he has ached with me the hundred times I have cried out to him. He understood that no matter how much she loved her God, there was still a deep aching in her because she didn't have a child.

As she poured out her anguish to the Lord, she worshipped. After she poured out her sorrow, she worshipped in a different way. Even before he gave her a child, she worshipped. And then he answered her. He gave her a son. He is the God who hears. And just as Hannah said in her prayer, "He is the God who knows."

Like Hannah, it is valid for us to say, "I don't believe this is my fault. It is something I don't understand. And it aches so much, Lord. Please, please, hear my cry. But in the midst of this trial, I still choose to worship you."

Gratitude and grieving don't have to be mutually exclusive. We can be thankful while simultaneously allowing ourselves to mourn. We need a balance between these two things.

Sometimes, all we can do to get through the pain is let ourselves grieve. Cheryl Strayed says, "Nobody will protect you from your suffering. You can't cry it away or eat it away or starve it away or walk it away or punch it away or even therapy it away. It's just there, and you have to survive it. You have to endure it. You have to live through it and love it and move on and be better for it and run as far as you can in the direction of your best and happiest dreams across the bridge that was built by your own desire to heal."[4]

When God talks to me, he calls me *Katie Girl*. Writing that name makes me teary, because it brings to mind a lifetime of journeys I have walked with the Lord. I know my Father's heart when I hear that name. I remember how much he loves me when I hear that name.

The other day, I was journaling out what I was hearing from God, like a letter from him. It is something I often do when I need to hear his tender voice. I had just experienced a difficult rejection from someone I cared deeply about, and I was weeping much like Hannah wept. I asked him the question I have asked more than any other in my life: "Lord, why do my relationships end in a broken heart instead of in a covenant? Why has no one fallen in love with me in such a long time? It aches so much. It doesn't seem right."

This is what he said: "Katie Girl, you have been faithful to believe in my goodness even after a very long time of praying for a family. You are so strong and so patient. I am not letting go of you, love. You will not be left unrewarded for your faithfulness to me. I keep all of my promises."

He did not say, "Now, Kate, you aren't trusting me in this place." He did not say, "Look at all that you do have, Kate. Be grateful for heaven's sake!" He did not tell me that I was weak. He told me that I was strong. So strong that I refused to let go of him, just like Hannah did. That is what I needed to hear in that moment.

As my song "Love of My Life" says,

> You are strong even in your weakness
> Even then you're lovely
> You are strong because I see you holy
> When you're covered in my love
> I weep when you're reaching from me
> I weep 'cause you love me blind
> You're the one—the one I'd die for
> You're the love, the love of my life. [5]

God does not see me weak. Even when I am weeping bitterly, he sees me strong. He sees me beautiful. He does not mock my pain. He bends down to hold me when I cry. I would venture to say that he cries with me not only because he aches with me, but also because he is so proud of the way I have trusted him through this, the longest, hardest trial of my life. Because I have loved him without always understanding his ways. Like the song says, I have loved him blind.

In the same way, he loves us blind. He loves us even in our weakness. He steers his eyes to see past our questioning and our frustration and our ranting until he gets to the deepest part of us, the part that is trying so hard to believe, the part of us that is faithful.

If you are experiencing this kind of grief, I think God is looking upon you with mercy right now. He is giving you permission to grieve. He is giving you permission to have compassion on yourself and to know that you are experiencing a true, deep loss. Even if it is a "disenfranchised loss," it is a grief that is real and painful.

He sees you trying to trust him, and it means so much.

Tomorrow, after we have allowed ourselves time to mourn, it would be wise for us to wake up, take a shower, have coffee with some friends, eat a salad instead of a pint of Ben and Jerry's, and remember that life is still beautiful. If we don't choose to have balance, we will get really depressed. We don't want to be stuck in this grief on a constant basis. We don't want to rant forever.

In the meantime, we can crawl into our Daddy's lap, let him call us by name, and remember that he is the God who knows.

We need to let him sing this song to us:

> Lay your weary head down now
> Let me hold you, hold you like a little child
> You don't have to be strong
> I will be strong for you
> You don't have to say a word, love
> Being close to you is all I want
> Rest here in my love
> Till it's enough for you
> Be still and know
> Quiet your soul
> In this world you will have trouble
> But take heart—I have overcome
> I have overcome
> Let me hold you close and hold you still

Know I love you and I always will
You don't have to hold on
I will hold on to you
Be still and know
Quiet your soul.[6]

Kate's Corner of Wisdom

How to Make Decisions

1. Figure out your truth. Not anyone else's. Yours.

2. Ask yourself, "What would I do if I weren't afraid?"

3. Do the next right thing.

4

The Lonely Doll

I remember very clearly the first book I ever read. I was four years old and sitting on our yellow shag carpet next to a big picture window. It was early evening. My mom had checked out the book from the library earlier in the week, and I had already looked through it several times. Mom sat next to me and pointed to the words, sounding them out one by one. Something clicked in my mind; I suddenly understood what it meant to read. I had already learned the alphabet, but now I grasped that when I put letters together, they made words.

At the time, I didn't realize that what I had just learned would change my life. All I knew was that when I started sounding out the words by myself, my mom was so proud of me. In fact, on that first night before I went to bed, she gave me a piece of taffy as a reward for learning to read. Reading the words of that book and receiving that reward is my most vivid memory from that age.

The main character of the book was a little doll named Edith. I vaguely remember that the doll lived in a big house and was very lonely. More than anything in the world, she wanted friends. I remember her being blonde and pretty, with little hoop earrings, and I remember that she had the same look on her face in every picture.

You see, Edith was a real doll, and the pictures of her weren't drawn but photographed. She was placed in poses around the author's house and all over New York, and the author used the pictures to weave stories together. The photographs made Edith seem so real, as if the stories were not mere make-believe. As if the doll could have been my next-door neighbor. As if I could have knocked on her door and said, "I'm lonely sometimes too. Let's be friends."

What I realize now is that I didn't just learn how to read that day, I learned what to expect. Words make stories. Stories shape beliefs. Beliefs shape lives. The words of that little storybook had me believing at a very young age that if I did things right, I would have a happy ending in which I wasn't lonely anymore, just like the lonely doll.

A few weeks ago, I was thinking about the book and how much it influenced me. I wondered if I could hunt it down online, but I could not remember the name of the author or even the title of the book. A few days later, one of my favorite radio programs, *This American Life*, aired a story about Dare Wright, a children's book author who was at the height of her fame in the late 1950s. The story discussed Miss Wright's life and how it paralleled the stories that she wrote. Within a few minutes I realized that the book they were talking about—her most famous book—was my book, the first book I had ever read. It was called *The Lonely Doll*. I was fascinated, and I went home to do more research.[1]

I discovered that Dare was a beautiful but troubled woman. She got engaged after a five-year courtship, but her fiancé called off the wedding, and soon after doing so he died in a plane crash. Dare was so devastated that she spoke out loud to pictures of him the rest of her life.

Soon after his death, Dare took pictures of her childhood doll and wrote these little stories. She changed the doll to look more like herself: straight blonde hair in a low ponytail and hoop earrings like she always wore and clothes similar to her own. Dare's method of easing her mourning was brilliant: She created a character that looked just like herself—a character who was as lonely as she was—and then she gave that character a happy ending.[2]

In the story, Little Edith, the doll, "lived in a nice house and had everything she needed except somebody to play with." She lived in New York, just like the author. Edith begged two pigeons on the windowsill to be her friends, but they flew away.

Edith knelt at her bed and, "Every night when she said her prayers, she pleaded, 'Please, please send me some friends.'" Soon the little doll's prayers were answered as two real-life stuffed F.A.O. Schwartz teddy bears moved in with her: a papa bear and a brother bear. And with these two new companions, Edith was not alone anymore.[3]

I related to the little doll just like the author did. I too was aching with loneliness.

My elementary school days were especially lonely. During that time, my parents went through a very difficult divorce. So difficult, in fact, that twenty-five years later they still didn't like being in the same room. My little heart shattered at their divorce. My parents have been attentive at different points of my life, but during the divorce they themselves were struggling with so much pain that they didn't seem to know how to deal with mine.

My school life was almost as difficult as my home life. I was a shy little girl. Recess was the worst time of the day for me because it reminded me that I was alone. I would wander around the playground aimlessly, trying to pass the time. I remember standing on the hill overlooking my classmates, all of whom didn't look very lonely, moving my thrift store coat zipper up and down and praying. It was a prayer very similar to Edith's prayer: "Please, please send me some friends. I don't want to be lonely anymore."

Now that I am an adult, my childhood prayer has been answered a hundredfold. I have had incredible friends in my life. I have spiritual parents who have nurtured me and who have talked with me when I was going through breakups or depressions. I have had countless strangers take me in while I was on music tours, who have fed me and who have taken time out of their schedules to get to know me. I have had friends who have brought me meals and knee-high socks to comfort me, friends who went shopping for me and cried with me when I was sick.

But I have a new thing I ask God for that hasn't been answered yet.

I stand on the hill overlooking my life. I move the zipper up and down on my fashionable black winter jacket. I look at the people below me with their careers and their spouses and their Facebook pictures of their beautiful children.

"Please, please send me a family," I pray. "I don't want to be lonely anymore."

I forget that I have friends and family all around me because I am so focused on the faraway people and their seemingly perfect lives. I compare my insides with their outsides, a comparison that is never helpful or accurate.

People always smile in pictures, but that doesn't mean that they are actually happy in real life. If I were to stop feeling so sorry for myself and climb down that hill, I would realize that their lives aren't perfect either. I would probably discover that many of these people are often lonely like me. We might even be able to comfort each other in our loneliness.

Stories like *The Lonely Doll* are told to us over and over again, first as children and then as adults. In the same radio story that talked about Dare Wright, there was an interview with long-time kindergarten teacher and author Vivian Paley. Dr. Paley has extensively studied the stories children make up. In it, she says that when young children are asked to tell a story, they usually say something like, "There was a little rabbit that lived in the woods and he was very lonely. Then a fox came and became friends with the rabbit and they weren't lonely anymore." And then the next child will say something like, "There was a car that was very very lonely. Then a truck came along and became the car's friend. They played together and then they weren't lonely."

According to Paley, the children tell different versions of this same story again and again. And interestingly, the listening children don't say, "Enough already! Why do you keep telling the same story?" Instead, they say, "More, more!"[4]

Clearly, even at a young age we don't like being alone. Even as children we understand that we were made for relationship. God designed it that way. We were born into families in which someone else has to care for us in order for us to survive. But we also recognize at an early age that our relationships are fragile and can be easily broken. We understand firsthand that we can suffer rejection and loneliness.

As children we sense that loneliness and disconnect are not good, so we want stories about little lonely characters meeting someone who loves them. Then as adults we hear this same story, only in a different form, again and again. There is a good reason that we are told the story so many times: It makes a lot of money.

In *The War of Art*, Steven Pressfield discusses the motto of a big advertising agency: "Invent a disease. Come up with the disease, and we can sell the cure."[5] I don't think it would be a stretch to say that Hollywood has greatly benefited from a disease called loneliness. They have sold a cure, and it is called romance.

Here is a sampling of the stories that have been told to us as adults:

Once upon a time in the 1980s, there were two lonely people named Harry and Sally. They hated each other at first, but later they became best friends. Then they had a big fight. Then they fell in love and they weren't lonely anymore.

Next story:

Once upon a time in the 1990s, a sleepless man in Seattle talked about being a lonely widower on a radio show. A cute, lonely blonde girl (who looked remarkably like Sally) decided she was madly in love with him, even though she had never met him. Then they met on top of the Empire State Building and they weren't lonely anymore.

And the next story:

Once upon a time in the 2000s, two lonely people who looked remarkably like the characters in the last story anonymously e-mailed each other very clever love letters. Neither one realized they were enemies in real life. They figured out that they loved each other, and then they weren't lonely anymore. (They seemed to have forgotten that they already met each other ten years ago on top of the Empire State Building.)*

Do you see how similar these movie plots are to the children's stories Dare Wright wrote and Dr. Paley observed? The lonely doll has been replaced by lonely adult men and women who find each other and have happy endings. We are told this story over and over again and we never seem to get tired of it. We clap our hands and say, "More, more!"

It would be wise for us to recognize our disease of loneliness and realize that getting married will not cure that disease. Real life is nothing like storybooks or chick flicks. There are no producers to come up with a predictable plot. No editors to cut out the parts you don't like. There are no writers who will answer every question and bring resolution to every challenge.

Your life won't have a perfectly hemmed-in ending. It will be ripped and tattered and re-sewn like a patchwork quilt. Marriage, singleness, divorce, loneliness, joy—these are the pieces of fabric that might make up that quilt. Whether God is the one who created the hard patches is not a question I can answer. But I do believe this: God is the thread. Your life is stitched with the color of his mercy, his grace, his love.

You may never understand why you are lonely on this earth. But

---

* These are the plots of the films *When Harry Met Sally*, *Sleepless in Seattle*, and *You've Got Mail*, respectively.

one day, God will hold out that quilt for you, and he will say, "Look what I made for you. Isn't it beautiful?" Then he will wrap the quilt around you, hold you close, and say, "There you go, love. You don't have to be lonely anymore."

That, my friends, will be the ending to your story. It is the happiest one of all.

5

The Trouble with Expectations

The other night, I rode my bike to the library of my charming Colorado town. It was perfect outside. The sun was setting and there was a street fair two blocks away from the library, complete with outdoor roller skating.

The library closed at 6 p.m., like it does every Friday. I went hoping to do some research, but I got there too late and was disappointed to find it closed. My expectations weren't met. I expected to be inside reading something riveting, but because it was closed, I had to sit on a bench with a laptop perched on my knees near the front doors of the library. My disappointment quickly dissipated, however, because it was so lovely outside.

As I sat there writing, though, something intriguing happened before my eyes. One by one people approached the automatic doors and waited for them to open. They realized the library was locked, they looked at the sign on the window—the closed sign, mind you—and they walked away, clearly disappointed. A little girl started crying because she wanted to have story time with her mom. A teenager cussed under his breath. A little boy who had to use the bathroom started whining. I counted nine people who expected to go to the library but couldn't get in. None of them could do anything about the locked doors, and none of them liked it. I wondered if this happened every Friday night.

As if on cue, a tall man with long white hair and a yellow T-shirt came to the door of the library with books in hand. The automatic doors didn't open, and he said out loud, "What?!" Then he started yelling over and over again, "What?! What?!" He was mad. I mean *really* mad. He walked back and forth in a rage right in front of me.

Dude, it's a library. There's a book drop twenty feet away. It will be open again at 9 a.m. Put your books in the book drop, go down the street, and enjoy the fair.

It seems pointless to get angry at a little thing like the library being closed. But this is what happens when you are consumed by unmet expectations. If you're not careful, your expectations will steal away your joy.

In many ways, I look as ridiculous as this man. I come to the library and look at the stories I wanted to write with my life. The story I dreamed of as a little girl, of friends coming and rescuing me from my loneliness. The story I wanted as a teenager, of a close-knit family rescuing me from my loneliness. The story I pray for as an adult, of a man who deeply loves me, rescuing me from my loneliness.

I stand at the doors of these expectations and they are locked.

"What?! What?!" I yell. "I want in! Why are these doors closed? This is not what I expected! This is not what I thought life would look like! I am outside the doors, and I am lonely. What do I do with this loneliness? With this emptiness?"

The hard truth is that even if I walk through those locked doors and over the threshold of marriage, I will struggle with disappointment. In fact, the more unrealistic my expectations about marriage, the more disappointed I will probably be.

My friend Tim said to me the other day, "Kate, if there is one thing I can guarantee about being married and having children, it's that it won't be anything like you expected."

I want to clap my hands over my ears and say, "No, no! Don't tell me that!"

But I would be wise to take my hands off my ears and listen to what he says, to realize that it is practically guaranteed that our lives will look much different from what we expect. I mean, when has life ever come about in the way you expected it to?

We create stories about what romance and marriage will look like. Stories are not necessarily bad things; they have been a central part of every culture since the beginning of time. But we live in a society where the stories we create do not give us a realistic view of what life in covenant looks like. We have to be careful about what we do with the expectations our made-up stories create.

If you are like me and have watched 1,246 chick flicks, you have started to think that the boy-meets-girl formula is the answer you've been looking for since you were a child. You have believed that the loneliness will be gone when you fall in love and get married, just like it was for Harry and Sally, with their wedding cake that has chocolate sauce on the side. With every story you hear, you have built up more expectation for what your own love story will look like.

In fact, I expect that the degree of resentment you may one day have in a marriage will be directly proportional to the unrealistic expectations that you have now.

In an article called "The Expectation Trap" in *Psychology Today*, author Hara Estroff Marano discusses how our culture has inundated us with the idea that all of our happiness can be found in our spouse. Marriage in other centuries was more centered around a woman being provided for and around raising a family than it was around love and intimacy. People attached a sense of duty rather than romance to marriage. Marano says,

> It wasn't until the 18th century that anyone thought that love might have anything to do with marriage. Because our intimate relationships are now almost wholly vehicles for meeting our emotional needs, and with almost all our emotions invested in one [person], we tend to look upon any unhappiness we experience whatever the

source—as a failure of a partner to satisfy your longings. Disappointment inevitably feels so personal. We see no other possibility but to hunt for individual psychological reason—that is, to blame our partners for our own unhappiness.

But much of the discontent we now encounter in close relationship is culturally inflicted, although we rarely interpret our experience that way. An accumulation of forces has made the cultural climate hostile to long-term relationships today.[1]

She goes on to say that our culture has created an atmosphere in which we feel the need to constantly monitor our own happiness. When we are not happy, we blame our lack of happiness on our spouse or on other people around us. We don't often look to ourselves or to what we have contributed to the dysfunction.

In the same article, William Doherty, professor of Family Sciences at the University of Minnesota, agrees: "People work themselves up over the ordinary problems of marriage, for which, by the way, they usually fail to see their own contributions. They badger their partners to change, convince themselves nothing will budge, and so work their way out of really good relationships."[2]

This is the trouble with expectations. If we are not careful, we will set ourselves up for disappointment and we may sabotage good relationships. We would do well to listen to the advice this doctor gives even before we are married—to work hard not to let our hopes be completely wrapped up in the person we may marry some day. To put boundaries on our expectations and not see marriage as a vehicle through which all of our needs will be met. That was never what marriage was meant to be.

I have had a few married friends tell me they experienced a new kind of loneliness after a few years of marriage. When they were single, the sentiment was, "When I get married, this aching in me will be filled." When they got married, it became, "I am married now, and this aching in me is still not filled. If this doesn't fill it, what will?" This doesn't happen in all marriages, but it does happen, and it is something we should prepare ourselves for.

Let's look at what Jesus says about expectations in Matthew 6:25-34:

> Therefore I tell you, do not worry about your life, what you will eat or drink; or about your body, what you will wear…Look at the birds of the air; they do not sow or reap or store away in barns, and yet your heavenly Father feeds them. Are you not much more valuable than they? Who of you by worrying can add a single hour to his life? And why do you worry about clothes? See how the lilies of the field grow. They do not labor or spin. Yet I tell you that not even Solomon in all his splendor was dressed like one of these. If that is how God clothes the grass of the field, which is here today and tomorrow is thrown into the fire, will he not much more clothe you, O you of little faith! So do not worry, saying, "What shall we eat?" or "What shall we drink?" or "What shall we wear?" For the pagans run after all these things, and your heavenly Father knows that you need them. But seek first his kingdom and his righteousness, and all these things will be given to you as well. Therefore do not worry about tomorrow, for tomorrow will worry about itself. Each day has enough trouble of its own.

Notice that Jesus doesn't say, "It would be a good idea not to worry about tomorrow." He says, "Do not worry about tomorrow." He commands it. Jesus is not really into projecting futures. Instead, he tells us to be present today, grateful for the people in your life at this moment, holding them closely and with love but holding them with open hands. Trust God with your future without expecting your future to look a certain way.

I am learning to take my life one day at a time rather than projecting all my hope onto a distant future. When that distant future comes, even if it involves a happy marriage, I probably won't feel that much more satisfied than I do today.

As Henri Nouwen states in his book *The Wounded Healer*, "We easily relate to our human world with devastating expectations. We ignore what we already know…that no love or friendship, no intimate embrace or tender kiss, no community, commune or collective, no man or woman, will ever be able to satisfy our desire to be released from our lonely condition."[3]

So if we aren't able to place our expectations for happiness in marriage, what should we put our hope in?

I know that the pat answer is to hope in God. Indeed, I have loved God for a very long time. I cannot deny for a second that he has given me hope, joy, and meaning. Knowing him has saved me from a life of abuse and despair. I will never fully know how my relationship with him has affected my life until I am in heaven.

But sometimes, even though I have the constancy of this hope, I still feel a deep ache. Life doesn't always feel right to me. When someone I love is sick, when I am around my street friends who have lived such hard lives, when I am having a bad day and just want someone to hold me, when a friend goes through a divorce, when I can barely look at a child without wanting to cry, life doesn't feel right. Because it's not right. We are longing for heaven. The hard truth is, God never promised that we wouldn't have seasons of aching in this life.

But he did promise us this: "'Though the mountains be shaken and the hills be removed, yet my unfailing love for you will not be shaken nor my covenant of peace be removed,' says the LORD, who has compassion on you" (Isaiah 54:10).

This is not some vague thought. It is a promise. No matter what happens, his love for us will not be shaken. That is something that is perfectly reasonable to hope in, because it is guaranteed.

I might be single for a long time—maybe for the rest of my life. I might love people who end up leaving me. I might get sick. People I care about could die. But no one, nothing, can take away the love God has for me. Ever. That may not be a truth that will completely take away my feelings of loneliness. But it is, nevertheless, a truth that gives me a reason to live.

Maybe I should stop focusing on the locked doors and go down the street to the fair instead. To the place that is not locked to me. To the place that is near to me at this very moment. It's possible that I will get to go into the library tomorrow, but today, I should stand in wonder at the beautiful sunset outside of those locked doors.

I want to move beyond expectations to a place of acceptance. Beyond unrealistic stories to a place of deeper, richer realities. Beyond loneliness to a place of rest and joyful solitude.

I would be wise to stop looking for my happy ending and start living in my happy today.

Kate's Corner of Wisdom

How to Have a Promising Future

1. Try to look at the fruit of something when it is still a seed.

2. Do the next right thing.

6

Confession, Reality TV, and the Space in Between

I have a secret to tell you. It is a secret I have told only a few of my closest friends. It is such a stunning secret that I never even hinted at it to my last boyfriend, and I told him pretty much everything about my life. But not this. I knew that his view of me would change if I told him.

Before I confess this secret to you, let me explain that minor panic sets in whenever I hear the word *confession*. This goes back many years to my Catholic upbringing.

I really didn't like going to Mass when I was a kid, which is the Catholic word for the weekly service. My love for God didn't accompany the tradition at the time, and so the services didn't often come alive for me. I didn't like saying the same words over and over again. I didn't like the kneeling and getting up and kneeling and getting up, like a room full of unsmiling jack-in-the-boxes.

My brother and I would try desperately to make the long hour of Mass pass more quickly. We would hold our breath, timing each other to see who could hold it the longest. We would draw little faces on our fingers and put on puppet shows, trying not to laugh.

We even had a special secret handshake for the part of the service when everyone shakes hands and says, "Peace be with you."

My brother set a bulletin on fire once. Definitely made that particular Mass less boring.

The thing I dreaded the most about being Catholic was not the Mass, however. It was confession. You know, like in the movies where you go behind a screen and tell the priest all of your deepest darkest sins. Except we didn't have a screen. We had to look Father Murphy straight in the face.

It was terrifying.

I had a secret back then too; one that I was scared of confessing. I was a kleptomaniac. I would go in a store with used grocery bags in my coat, fill a basket with makeup and chocolates, go into the bathroom, put the loot in the bags, and walk out of the store. It was brilliant, really. I stole so many chocolates that to this day, I can tell you the filling of any Russell Stover chocolate just by their shape. My brothers and I would also use this method to steal key lime pies and eat them in the parking lot.

I remember standing in the line for confession, wondering what to do. Should I tell the priest that I stole everything I could get my hands on, including things like a $1,500 pearl necklace from the people I babysat for? How would I tell him? Would eight Hail Marys really absolve what I had done? Should I just skip confessing this particular sin and pretend that I was a better person than I really was?

I remember the conversation going like this: "Forgive me, Father, for I have sinned." Cue lots of crying on my part. "I steal things. Mostly sugary things. My mom doesn't let us have sugary things, and I just can't help myself. I love truffles! I love key lime pie! I would give up the key lime pie, Father, but not the chocolates. Please, please, don't make give up the chocolates!"

(Side note: As an adult, I still have a minor obsession with chocolate, but now my tastes have been refined to really good dark chocolate. I buy it with my hard-earned money instead of sticking it in my coat, though, just in case you were wondering.)

My Catholic upbringing was the first leg of my faith journey. I have had many adventures along the way since then, and each part of the path has brought me through a variety of different denominations. Over the years, I have been a member of conservative community churches, Evangelical-Free-turned-ultra-charismatic churches, house churches, and edgy, artsy social justice churches. I honestly don't know about the doctrines of any of these denominations; I just know that I love Jesus and that I look for family wherever I am.

However, in the last few years I have found a new depth and resonance for my faith in the same place I started this journey: in ancient traditions and mystical ponderings that mimic those of the Catholic faith. I have a newfound love for these ancient traditions, and they have become a rich part of my recent spiritual life.

I credit this new love to an internship I did with InnerChange. InnerChange is my favorite organization I have worked with, and I am praying about working with them full-time. I worked with one team in San Francisco whose goal was to minister to young homeless people in Golden Gate Park. I befriended street kids and ate meals with them in our home. I taught a music class with young homeless people and made an album of their music. Our team chose to be homeless for three days in order to understand better what life on the streets is like. It was one of the most eye-opening experiences of my life.

In InnerChange, each missionary patterns the rhythm of his or her life in traditionally monastic ways, making sure there is rest and fellowship built into the week so no one gets burnt out with the ministry work. Each missionary goes on solitary retreats every six months to either a monastery or to a hermitage. (Yes, there are still hermits. In fact, the hermit I met at Sky Farm Hermitage in California was one of the warmest people I've ever met. Her life consists of hosting guests, gardening, praying for peace, and saying wonderful, wise things in a voice like a Disney princess. She's beautiful.)

Since interning with InnerChange, I have made visiting monasteries and hermitages a part of my lifestyle. I've visited five monasteries from Ireland to Colorado to Big Sur, California, in the last two years. These monasteries are beautiful, serene places where I can set apart time to listen to God. To hear his heartbeat. I love it.

After many years of going to churches that were worried about having one smidgen of silence in their services, I have been refreshed by the quietness of contemplation. I have loved feeling like I can come to God and be silent with him. I have loved just letting him love me. My faith journey has seemed to come full circle when it comes to denominations. Back to the deep faith of an ancient church.

All of that—the reading, the retreating, the working, the contemplating—is a part of me that I especially like. The part that deeply loves Jesus and deeply loves people who are hurting, not to mention the part that is cool enough to be homeless for a few days. In my mind, you now know the "good" part of me. The part that I think will impress you.

I would like to make you believe that the deep, beautiful, mystical Kate is who I am all the time. To convince you there is no such person as the weak, insecure Kate.

But your view of me is about to change, because the dreaded confession that I mentioned is coming. Right now, my bedroom is like the confession room and my MacBook Pro is my virtual Catholic priest and our conversation might go something like this: "Forgive me, Father MacBook Pro, for I have sinned." I pour out my heart to the screen and it responds, "Your sin has been absolved, my daughter. Buy three iPhone apps and live in peace."

Making this confession is especially scary to me, because you are now going to know a part of me I don't like very much.

Okay. Here I go. Here is my secret: I watch *The Bachelor*.

"Are you kidding?" you say. "All this talk of childhood kleptomania and a Catholic confession digression and Russell Stover...you're going to write all of that to lead up to your deepest darkest secret and it's watching a TV show? I thought we would get something really gossip-worthy, like that you were secretly dating a Brazilian diplomat or that you're a double agent or something."

But you see, watching *The Bachelor* makes me feel like I am much shallower than I make myself out to be. I honestly would rather have admitted that I used to be a drug dealer. You just read about how I worked with this incredible organization helping street kids. You read about how I have become much more of a centered person. You read about how I spend time meditating and having solitude retreats and meeting hermits and monks. But now that you know the truth, you won't remember any of the good stuff; you will only remember me as that author girl who shallowly watches *The Bachelor*.

A person who watches *The Bachelor*? Not mystical. She's one step up from a soap opera addict.

I think I have felt especially secretive about watching this show because for most of my adult life, I haven't been a big TV watcher. I grew up watching too much TV, so when I got older, I kind of hated it. I looked at people who always had the TV on and thought of them as lazy. I was better than them. I read books instead of watching television. I wasn't going to give in to popular culture—not now, not ever. I would not be materialistic. I would not listen to Top 40 pop songs—they aren't hip enough for me. I would be countercultural. I would be deep. I would be a super-non-TV-watching-got-over-my-kleptomania-intriguing-indie-music-listening-mystical-social-justice-loving-follower-of-Jesus-who-wears-Toms-shoes.

But during the last few years, when I was in ministry school and being taught about spiritual things all the time, when I was working with homeless people and feeling so sad for them, when I was touring and meeting so many people that I was sapped of all my energy, well, sometimes I just wanted to stop thinking.

During these difficult seasons, I realized that I could have TV on my own laptop and hide it a little more. It became less of a social event and more of a private event. So I started watching it. And *The Bachelor* became my one staple TV show.

I know, I know. If I'm going to watch one show, why would I choose this one? It is just ridiculous. Every season is the same. The man with the perfect chest and perfect charm. The synthetically-endowed, bikini-wearing, bleached-hair-perfect, gorgeous women. Some of them are sweet; some of them are psycho. In fact, I heard a radio program in which a reality show producer admitted to trying to cast forty percent narcissists and people who are crazy enough to make good television but not crazy enough to bash the camera in with a bat.

Every season the same scenes repeat over and over throughout the episode ("Next, on *The Bachelor*…") so they can fill two hours and get a lot of money from advertisers. There are the same make-out sessions with a boatload of girls. And there is always the same saga of the man being totally torn by his deep love for two (or three or four) women, all of whom he's known for about five weeks. And host Chris Harrison always, always says, "And now, for the most shocking ending in *The Bachelor* history." I mean, it's ridiculous.

And for some mysterious reason, I love every minute of it.

I admit I have a problem. *Why?* I ask myself. *Why would I want to watch this show?*

In order to feel less shallow, I like to tell myself that I'm not just watching TV; I am observing a sociological experiment. I ask myself with a very scientific air, "What is the psychological process of a man who is put into a room with a number of beautiful women? When he has to choose who he wants to break up with and who he wants to keep?" I convince myself that I'm a lot like Jane Goodall, only instead of watching chimps and the way they interact, I'm observing a bunch of hot people.

I'm not watching this for entertainment, people! I'm watching it for research! Under my blanket and with my headphones on, so my housemates won't hear the mumbling of romantic TV encounters coming from under the door. What's wrong with that?

I am learning that other people share this secret. Recently, I mentioned a character on *The Bachelor* to one of my best friends and covered my mouth when I realized my mistake.

"You watch *The Bachelor*?" she asked.

Sheepishly, I replied, "Yes, yes I do," as if I were admitting to being a kleptomaniac or something.

"I do too!" she said.

"What?"

"I've always watched it in secret because I was afraid of what people would think of me if they knew."

"Me too!"

"Are you kidding? We could have been watching it together this whole time!"

I've met more and more people with the same secret addiction, even married couples who are pastors. Maybe we can all get together and create a support group or something where I could ease my conscience by saying "Hi, I'm Kate, and I am a Bacheloraholic."

So there. I've said it. I've told you my secret. It's out in the open. I feel absolved. Thank you, Father MacBook Pro. Thank you.

I feel surprisingly good about telling you my secret. I think I feel so good because I am not trying to hide anything anymore. There is something freeing about sharing both the good, deep, beautiful parts and the shallow, selfish parts of myself with you.

Obviously, I have struggles that are much deeper than my love for *The Bachelor*. I struggle with striving for attention. I often put too much hope in people I date and end up smothering them if I'm not careful. I am not always a good listener. I struggle with being happy in the moment and I wish for the past or for the future far too often. Sometimes I am terrified of getting older. I can be self-absorbed and selfish at times.

When I focus on these shortcomings, I believe the lie that if people really knew me, they wouldn't like me. To combat this lie, I have to learn to accept myself like God does. The more I accept myself, the more I will be able to accept love from other people. And when I accept myself, I will also be better at loving others in their weakness.

I want to pattern my love for myself, for my potential spouse, for my friends, and for my future children after God's love. God's love is very special. On one hand, he wants us to move from "glory to glory"—to deeper levels of wholeness (2 Corinthians 3:18 NKJV). But he also loves us in our imperfections right now, where we are today—whether we're diving into his word at a monastery or watching way too many episodes of reality TV.

As Graham Cooke says, "There is nothing you can do that would make him love you more. There is also nothing you can do to make him love you less. He loves you because he loves you, because he loves you, because he loves you, because that is what he is like...It is his nature to love, and you will always be the beloved. He won't love you any better when you become better...He loves all the way, all the time."[1]

For much of my life I have been scared to show people my imperfections. I often show only the perfect parts of myself. I have hated my imperfections, wondering if those explain why I have been rejected in my life. But now I want to love myself and others with the kind of love God loves me with.

Keeping up appearances can be completely exhausting. I don't want to hide "imperfect me" from the world anymore. And even though I consistently want to work to become a more healthy person, I also want to be accepting of today's imperfect me. I am a great big ball of compassion and contemplation and insecurities and *Bachelor* watching and spiritual depth and losing things and quirky humor and deep love for people. I am a mix of good and bad. I am far from perfect. But imperfect me is infinitely valuable and lovable not only to God, but to other people. To myself.

The person I may marry one day will also be a ball of wonderful and difficult, just like I am. But I want to love someone like that. I don't want the fairy tale anymore. I want something real. I want someone real.

When I watch *The Bachelor*, I see the flowers and the helicopter rides and the beautiful destinations and the beaches and the bikinis, and I am not in the least bit jealous. I understand that is not what love is. Romantic love, like the "love" found on *The Bachelor*, is a lot like fireworks, momentarily beautiful but not anything that will last forever. When the fairy tale is no longer staged and the camera stops rolling, there is not a lot of relationship left. It can happen with reality shows, and it can also happen with real-life romances. That is not what I want.

Real love takes hard work. It takes years and even decades of striving to understand and accept someone, imperfections and all. Real relationships are made up of hundreds of hours of building a history together. If you get married someday, you will not just be married to the person, you will be married to the history that you have built with that person.

As Henri Nouwen says, "Marriage is not a lifelong attraction of two individuals to each other, but a call for two people to witness together to God's love. The basis of marriage is not mutual affection, or feelings, or emotions and passions that we associate with love, but a vocation, a being elected to build together a house for God in this world, to be like the two cherubs whose outstretched wings sheltered the Ark of the Covenant and created a space where Yahweh could be present."[2]

If I do get married, my husband will most likely love me more than he loves anyone else in the world. But there will still be times when he hurts me. I will often think there is no one as wonderful as him anywhere. But there will be other times when I'll be annoyed by him. My job will not be to judge if he is good enough for me. My job will be to love him well. We will build a history together. We will build together a house for God in this world.

Thomas Merton said, "The beginning of love is to let those we love be perfectly themselves, and not to twist them to fit our own image. Otherwise, we love only the reflection of ourselves we find in them."[3]

At this point, I haven't just given up on meeting a perfectly chested bachelor. I've given up on wanting anyone who is perfect. I want a real, breathing person. I don't want someone who is ideal, just someone who is a deal. (Okay, I know that's cheesy. But it might very well make a lot of money as a magnet sold at marriage conferences.)

If I get married, my spouse will be real and he will be hard to live with at times. But that is okay because I will be real too, and I will be hard to live with at times too. When I don't expect my mate to be ideal, I won't expect myself to be ideal. I will feel more free to be the imperfect me. I won't need to hide anymore. I won't need to have secrets. I can confess things and not be afraid that it will make me unlovable.

Even now, while we are single, it is important to love our friends and family for who they are, not for who we want them to be.

As my friend Brandon says, marriage should not be about finding a perfect person who will meet all of your needs. Marriage should be about creating a room where both of you can be human.

And I wouldn't mind a room in which I am occasionally allowed to watch reality television.

The Case for Thankfulness

If the only prayer you said in your whole life
was 'thank you,' that would suffice."

Meister Eckhart[1]

A few days ago I rode my bike along the Coal Creek trail, which is about thirty feet from my house. It was the end of September and my favorite time of year in Colorado. The weather for my ride was perfect. The air smelled like a mixture of dying leaves and honeysuckle. The sun was lighting up the rustic scenery like an ethereal baptism. I could hear the rush of the creek beside me, and it sounded like hope.

But there were gnats. Lots and lots of gnats. Like, millions of them. I enjoyed the ride until I would hit pockets of the tiny little nuisances. They would smack me in the face like a sultry woman in a bad soap opera.

I kept thinking, *Dang it! This ride would be perfect if it weren't for the gnats.* The little insects were all I could think about the whole ride. I even debated in my head why a good God would create such annoying bugs that often ruin my outdoor experiences.

To escape the gnats, I stopped at my "J" tree by the water. The J tree is, as expected, a tree that looks like a J.

I leaned against my tree, away from the gnats, and breathed deep.

I started thinking about how good it felt to be able to ride a bike—let alone one that was given to me for free—and how good it felt to have this breathtaking landscape sitting thirty feet behind my house, waiting for me to explore it. Then I thought about my body, which had been in constant pain and exhaustion only a few years ago when I was sick with Lyme disease. There is no way that I could have ridden a bike in that terrible season. I could barely walk down the street.

The thing I prayed for more than anything else during that time was for my body to be healthy. It was a desperate, hopeless prayer. I honestly didn't think it would ever be answered.

But here I was, sitting on my J tree, just breathing. I was incredibly healthy with no constant pain in my joints, with no exhaustion, and with a full night's sleep every night for the last week. And I was able to ride my bike.

I breathed in deep the air of God's goodness.

My prayer for health had been answered in abundance. But with the challenges and the busyness of the days since my healing, I had forgotten that God had answered that prayer. Sitting by the water, breathing in the crisp air, I remembered. And I was thankful.

On my ride back, I smiled more than I've smiled in a long time.

I quickly realized that smiling isn't the best decision when you are surrounded by gnats, and I reminded myself to floss when I got home.

After my bike ride, I was taught another lesson about thankfulness through my hunt for a new tent.

I have been looking for a new tent for a while. My current thirty-two dollar Target tent has a rainfly that looks a little like an Asian hat and barely covers the screened roof. Every time I go camping, I wonder why the weather is always such that I carefully have to direct the puddles on my floor away from the space where I'm sleeping. It probably has less to do with the weather and more to do with my cheapo tent.

I've used that tent for five summers, so I've been looking for a new one for months now. Avoiding hypothermia may very well be worth spending a few more dollars.

In hot pursuit of my modern tabernacle in the wilderness, I found a tent on Craigslist that was perfect for me. Great reviews, light, waterproof, three season, right size. And forty bucks. Score!

I excitedly called the seller. He told me that he had just sold the tent to someone else. I was really disappointed. I started mulling over in my head how much I wanted that tent.

A few hours later I went to the streets to play music with some friends. I was shivering quite a bit because I had lost my winter coat on a plane. My friend said, "I have a coat I can give you! I was going to give it away anyway." I walked with her to her house, and she gave me a perfect, almost-new, expensive North Face ski jacket.

Now, at the end of the day, can you guess what I was thinking about? I'll give you one hint: It had everything to do with a tent and nothing to do with a coat.

God was probably up there saying, "Hey, Kate! Did you like that really nice North Face coat I got you? You've been praying for that one!"

All I said was, "MAN! I wanted that tent."

As I lay in bed that night, I let my thoughts go even further down the road of discontent. I thought, "I can't believe I didn't get that tent. I'm going to get hypothermia for sure. I would have had perfect camping experiences for the rest of my life if I had only bought that tent."

I decided to throw a full-on pity party, which I often do. "I always come so close to getting something and then have it taken away from me. That's just how my life is. It doesn't just happen with tents, it happens with people too. Either they leave me or I lose them."

And then, the horrible thought crossed my mind that seems to lurk in the corners and pounce when I am not being careful: "I will always be alone."

This thought startled me. I realized that I went from "I didn't get a forty-dollar tent on Craigslist" to "I will always be alone" in the space of a few minutes. How did that happen?

I caught a glimpse of my new coat hanging in the closet, and I recognized my attitude of ungratefulness. I was given the gift of a wonderful bike ride, the remembrance of my health and my dear friends, and a great new coat to keep me warm. But all I could focus on was the tent I didn't get, which turned into thinking about the life I didn't have. I all but missed the beautiful gifts God gave me because I was focusing so much on what he hadn't given me.

Someone recently asked me what I would have left if I were to lose everything that I wasn't thankful for today. As I lay in bed, I thought about that and I was very humbled.

I sat up. I breathed in. I felt the air rush into my lungs. And I sincerely thanked God for my coat. For my bike ride. For my friends. For my health. I didn't beg him for the grandiose things he could give me tomorrow. I thanked him for the simple things he had already given me that day.

That seemed to make a way for God to walk into the room. He had been standing nearby the whole time; I just hadn't seen him before. But now I saw him. He kissed me on the head.

I looked up into his good, good face, and I said, "I'm sorry for forgetting you, Papa." He said, "That's okay, love. I'm still here."

That is the power of thankfulness. It prepares a way for God to come into the rooms of our heart so we can look at his good, good face.

We see a dramatic picture of the power of thankfulness in the story of Jehoshaphat, one of the kings of Judah in the Old Testament. He started his reign with great integrity, following in the footsteps of David. The Bible says, "His heart took delight in the ways of the LORD" (2 Chronicles 17:6 NKJV). Jehoshaphat's reign was blessed with God's mercy for a long time.

During this season, God's blessings surrounded Jehoshaphat like air. Often, however, like most of us, he took the air for granted. Jehoshaphat eventually stopped relying on God and started relying on his own ability to control things.

He began to make decisions without God—bad decisions. He decided to align himself with a powerful man named Ahab by arranging the marriage of his own daughter to Ahab's son. Yes, we're talking about Ahab, of Ahab and Jezebel fame. Probably the most notoriously evil couple in history.

Not necessarily the smartest choice for in-laws.

The alliance with Ahab soon brought disaster on Jehoshaphat's kingdom, and the king was confronted by the prophet Jehu about his unwise alliance. It was clear that King Jehoshaphat was nowhere near a place of delighting in the Lord anymore. He had stopped trusting in the Lord and had started trusting in his own political decisions. The near demise of his kingdom proved that that was a bad move.

Soon Judah's enemies, the Moabites, formed a powerful confederacy with the surrounding nations, and they planned to attack Jehoshaphat and his people. The enemy army was vast, and the people of Judah were terrified. People from every region in Judah assembled together to seek the Lord and hear Jehoshaphat's plan: "All the men of Judah, with their wives and children and little ones, stood there before the LORD" (2 Chronicles 20:13).

I want you to picture this scene for a moment. Jehoshaphat stands before all the people he rules over. He sees husbands and wives together with babies in their arms and toddlers at their feet. Jehoshaphat realizes that every person in front of him could potentially be killed because of his decision to control things rather than to trust in God. And now here they are, humbly praying with their king, looking to him for the decision that will determine if they live or die. He wants to make the right decision this time. He doesn't want these people to be destroyed.

So he lays down his manipulative ways, and he puts the future of his kingdom into God's hands.

He does not give the common battle speech: "Boys, we're going to get in there and we are going to destroy them!" Instead, he speaks honest words of desperation. He admits how weak they are. He says, "O, our God...we have no power to face this vast army that is attacking us. We do not know what to do; but our eyes are upon you" (2 Chronicles 20:12).

A messenger of the Lord comes and says, "Thus says the LORD to you: 'Do not be afraid nor dismayed because of this great multitude, for the battle is not yours, but God's.'" And then he says, "You will not need to fight in this battle. Position yourselves, stand still and see the salvation of the LORD, who is with you" (2 Chronicles 20:15,17 NKJV).

Listen close, dear readers, because this is, in my opinion, the most important part of the story.

In the morning, as they went out to battle, "Jehoshaphat appointed men to sing to the LORD and to praise him for the splendor of his holiness as they went out at the head of the army, saying: 'Give thanks to the LORD, for his love endures forever'" (2 Chronicles 20:21).

Consider what a ridiculous war tactic this would seem to be to the men in the army. They have come to fight a battle. Their lives are at stake. Their family's lives are at stake. Their wives may become widows after this day. Their children may become fatherless.

But they have sought the Lord together with their king. Their eyes are set on the Lord alongside their leader. So when Jehoshaphat appoints a worship team to march at the very front of the battle line, ahead of all the strong warriors, they do it. When he asks them to use songs of thankfulness to battle with instead of swords, they go out there and sing with all of their might.

This seems foolish. Did they really think that mere words, a mere attitude of the heart, was going to win a battle for them?

But that's exactly what happened. As the army marched forward praising God, the Moabites, who were still far off, started quarreling among themselves and ended up killing each other before Jehoshaphat's army even got there. Jehoshaphat's army didn't raise one sword. They didn't need to, because they lifted their praises instead.

Perhaps the Moabite army heard the praises of the people and got confused. The enemies were probably asking themselves, "How could they be praising God when they have so little hope that they are going to survive? Maybe there is something that we don't know! Maybe they are more powerful than we think they are!" Fear and chaos ensued.

The truth is, Jehoshaphat's army was thanking God in spite of their dire circumstances, and that is what ended up rescuing them. God said that they wouldn't have to fight this battle, and they didn't. Their gratitude fought the battle for them.

Likewise, the enemy is often not defeated by us battling with him, but he is often confused and defeated by thankfulness.

There are times I don't think I have any strength left in me to battle the loneliness of being single. There are times I don't think I can face the thought of not ever having a biological child. There are times I'm not sure if I can get through another night of slipping into my single bed alone. There are times that, like Jehoshaphat, I say in desperation, "I have no power to face this vast army that is attacking me! I do not know what to do!" But then I try to gather enough strength and wisdom to add, "but my eyes are on you."

Maybe I would be wise to choose, like Jehoshaphat, to fight the battle with the words, "Give thanks to the LORD, for his love endures forever."

When I choose to battle all the plaguing thoughts of loneliness with thankfulness, maybe I will hear the words of my Savior: "You do not need to fight this battle alone, Katie Girl. Stand still. See the salvation of your Lord. I'm still here."

I have been trying to deal with my discontent lately by waking up and saying these simple words over and over again: "Acceptance and gratefulness. Acceptance and gratefulness. Acceptance and gratefulness." Repeating this helps me drown out the mantra that I am more tempted to repeat: "Complaining and bitterness. Complaining and bitterness. Complaining and bitterness." I try to remember that the word *complain* comes from the same root word as *plaintiff*, meaning "someone who accuses." In fact, plaintiffs are also called *complainants*. By complaining, I am accusing God.

I don't want to do that. I want to be grateful. This is the day God has given me. Some of the hours are going to be hard, and some of them are going to be beautiful. It would be wise to accept my reality, whatever that may be, and live as fully as I can within that reality. Rather than waking up and saying, "How could this possibly be my life?" I want to be able to say, "This is the day that the LORD has made. Let us rejoice and be glad in it!" (Psalm 118:24).

When I thank God for this day he has given me, no matter how difficult it is, my heart will be freed up to behold God's abounding goodness that surrounds me like air every day. I will have serenity not because of my circumstances, but because of my thankfulness.

The power of thankfulness is so strong that it will go beyond helping me have a good day. It will help me have a good life. When I choose acceptance and gratefulness, many of the wounds I now bear will one day be scars gilded with gold.

To remind me of this truth, I have a vase full of stones that sits at my bedside. On every stone, I have affixed a picture. For every season I go through I have one stone with a picture on it that represents the season, and another stone and picture that represents what God taught me in that season.

During the depression I went through in college, symbolized by a picture of a girl crying, I learned that God would heal and restore me as many times as waves crashed to the shore, shown by a picture of a lighthouse.

During the season of my sickness, marked with a picture of a tick, I understood more what it meant to be loved and to depend on those that I love, represented with a picture of a girl holding a heart balloon.

After writing a letter extending forgiveness to someone who greatly hurt me, symbolized by a picture of a letter in a mailbox, I learned that God's forgiveness of me and my forgiveness of others puts me in a place where I can't be bound up by anything, which is represented by a picture of a girl with long red hair dancing with abandon.

I made these stones to be my Ebenezers, which, literally translated, means "stone of help" (1 Samuel 7:12). Ebenezer was the site at which the Israelites got the Ark of the Covenant back years after it was stolen. Samuel set up a stone memorial in that place and said, "Thus far, the LORD has helped us" (1 Samuel 7:12). He set it up as a way to pause and say, "God, we have been through a lot, but you have always been faithful. You have helped us before, and you will keep on helping us. Thank you for what you've done so far, and thank you for what you will keep on doing."

I look through my stones occasionally to remember that God has helped me through every season of my life. They remind me that he has rescued me before, and he will rescue me again. They bring me a great sense of gratitude for all that God has done for me.

These stones mark the trials I have gone through, but they also mark the wisdom gained, the life lived, and the trust for the one who never stops walking with me. If I keep walking this road with God, the hard trial I endure now will one day be a picture on a stone, marking the wisdom that God gave me in this part of my journey.

I will look at that stone and I will be grateful for this season, no matter how hard it was in the moment. That stone will help me remember that no matter what I go through, "God causes all things to work together for good to those who love God, to those that are called according to his purpose" (Romans 8:28 NASB).

As Jean Baptiste of Massieu said, "Gratitude is a memory of the heart." I remember today, God. I remember.

The Great
Name Changer

I am many things other than a single woman: lover of God, lover of people, traveler of the world, teacher, lover of the poor and downcast, avid reader, overcomer of a chronic disease, ridiculous enjoyer of dark chocolate and good cheese, lover of nature, worshipper. But "single" is often the only label I give myself.

The labels you give yourself and that others give you slowly build a path you follow, like water in the crevice of a rock. Unless you consciously direct the water somewhere else by believing what God says about you, you will flow wherever that label wants to take you.

For instance, constantly comparing yourself to magazine models might give you the idea that you are ugly. Believing that label could lead you down the road of low self-worth and eating disorders. If you grow up with a father who says you will never amount to anything, you may call yourself a failure and never attempt to get an education or a good job. If several people have broken up with you or cheated on you, you may label yourself as unlovable and, consequently, you may shy away from getting close to people so they won't reject you.

You will live out these labels unless you consciously replace them with your true identity. In the above cases, you could say, "I am not ugly; I am beautiful," "Failure is not my destiny; abundance is," or, "I am not unlovable; the more people get to know me, the more they love me." Regularly replacing the lies with the truth is crucial to living a life that is not determined by your past.

I want to share one of my favorite stories with you—a story that beautifully illustrates a group of people replacing an inaccurate label with their true identity.

A group of Latino immigrants lived in an apartment complex in the Westlake area of Los Angeles. The Latino tenants were labeled as "poor" and perhaps even "worthless," and so they were treated that way by their slum landlords. The living conditions were awful. The *Los Angeles Times* said that the apartments were one of the "worst slum disgraces in the city."[1] Cockroaches infested everything. The lights and showers often didn't work, the toilets were clogged, and there was a lake of sewage in the basement. Up to that point the tenants hadn't challenged their landlord's ill treatment of them. Perhaps they didn't believe they deserved any better. Soon there were open drug deals, shootings, and stabbings occurring inside the apartments.

A group of InnerChange missionaries decided to live out the gospel by moving into these horrible living conditions and loving their new neighbors well. The missionaries slowly became a trusted part of the community. Some of the tenants and missionaries had such a strong connection that they considered each other family. The InnerChange team helped the Latino immigrants remember that they were not merely poor; in God's eyes they were precious.

After a season, a group of the Latino tenants created a task force attempting to change their horrible living conditions. They met in the InnerChange apartments because they knew the missionaries would help guide them in their efforts.

Three Latina women, Teresa, Josefina, and Maria, became passionate advocates for their cause. The InnerChange team supported them, but the team did not take over. Together, they organized legal action against the owners of the apartment building. It took six years of fighting together, but all of the tenants eventually became co-op owners of the building. That had never happened before in the history of Los Angeles.

Toward the end of the effort to reclaim their homes, one of the men who lived in the complex was diagnosed with inoperable cancer. He held on long enough to walk with his family through the doors of his newly owned apartment, and he was so proud. It was the first time he had ever owned a home. Two days after moving in, he died. The tenants went door to door to collect money for the family. The place that had been filled with prejudice and murder was now a community.

Teresa, Josefina, and Maria have been given many awards, and they have even been flown to conferences to talk about how to bring dignity and justice to poor communities. One by one, these brave women are helping other poor people rise above their physical and emotional poverty.

There is incredible power in rising above your labels. This community went from believing they were worthless to believing they were valuable, from poor to homeowners, from adversaries to family. They were encouraged to believe in their true identity and throw out the labels people had put on them, and they did.[2]

Here's another story about labels. As a social experiment, billboards were put up in two different cities. The billboards had a picture of the same full-figured woman. One billboard said, "I think I'm fat. What do you think?" The other billboard said, "I think I'm beautiful. What do you think?"

A survey was then given for each city. About 80 percent of the people who saw the billboard that said, "I think I'm fat" thought the model was fat. Likewise, 80 percent of the people who looked at the "I think I'm beautiful" billboard decided she was beautiful.

Who you believe you are changes everything.

The biblical story of Jacob illustrates this same idea—that you often become what you label yourself and what others label you.

In Hebrew culture, the firstborn son was given two different endowments: a birthright, which allowed him to take on his father's name in social and legal matters, and a double portion of the inheritance. The firstborn was a coveted position, and there is no clearer example of a man who coveted this position than Jacob.[3]

Jacob came out of the womb with his hand outstretched, grasping his twin brother Esau's heel, desperate to win in the race for firstborn. It seems that even in the first seconds of his life, Jacob was trying to control his own destiny. He was given the name Jacob, a name that means "deceiver," or "supplanter," which could also be interpreted as "one who wants to be what he is not."

Sound familiar?

Not surprisingly, the one who was given the name "deceiver" became one of the most notorious deceivers in the Bible. For most of his life, Jacob tried to reverse the birth order. His life was defined by this perceived injustice. To put it bluntly, Jacob wanted to be someone else so much that he became a control freak.

When Esau came in starving after hunting, Jacob offered food in exchange for his birthright. Later, Jacob pretended to be Esau when his father, Isaac, was dying so that he would receive the blessing—a double portion of the inheritance.

Jacob wasn't firstborn, but he thought he should have been. Maybe if he worked really hard at it, if he spent his life trying to change it, he could trick himself, his family, and even his God into believing that he was firstborn. Ironically, God had told his mother that "the older will serve the younger" (Genesis 25:23). All of this manipulation was for naught, as Jacob would have eventually been the one in authority even without his control freakish ways.

My trials look different from Jacob's. Jacob rehearsed over and over in his head that if he had been the firstborn, he would have had all that he wanted. I rehearse over and over in my head that if God would give me a husband that adores me, I would have all that I want. If I had children who loved the Lord, I would have all that I want. If my career flourished and people around the world listened to my music and read this book, I would have all that I want. If my relationships did not fail and I were never rejected, I would have all that I want.

I too want to be someone I am not. I know God understands this struggle, but I also know he doesn't want me to constantly mull over how unsatisfied I am with my life. He knows that when I do that, I am living as "one who wants to be who she is not."

I, like Jacob, often want God's promises sooner than he has given them to me. I want my right to marry, and I throw caution to the wind and say, "By God, I'm going to get it." But the truth is, if I try to manipulate God's promise, the fruit will be slavery rather than freedom. If I refuse God's help and try to do it on my own, if I become obsessed with figuring out how to get what I want when I want it, I will become a slave to my desires. I will sacrifice my peace for my expectations.

These control-freak tendencies can even look like godly practices sometimes. Maybe if I pray enough? Fast enough? If I let go enough? These actions turn into slavery if my motivation is to get what I want rather than to get closer to God.

I mourn when I think how I've treated God at times. This is my Jesus, who feels deeper and loves more passionately than anyone in the world. This is the one who has journeyed with me, who has comforted me and who has been faithful to me every second of my life. This is the one who bled and died so he could be near me when I ache for a husband.

And now, in my pain, I often reduce him to a genie in a bottle who grants me wishes if I rub the right way.

Forgive me, Lord, forgive me.

After Jacob stole the birthright and the father's blessing from his older brother, he married and lived many years in prosperity. One year, Jacob traveled with his family to Canaan. He heard news that Esau, whom he hadn't seen since he swindled him, was coming to meet him with an army of four hundred men. Terrified, Jacob sent gifts to Esau, hoping to ease the wrath his brother might bring against him.

That same night, he took his family to cross a river called Jabbok. Jabbok means "a place of emptying out," or "a place of passing over" and was a symbol of struggle to the Hebrew people.[4] Jacob sent his wives and possessions across the river and was left alone. What an incredible picture! The things he had schemed for—his inheritance and his family—were the things he needed to let go of in order to find his true identity.

As he watched the dreams he based his identity on fade away in the distance, he stood alone on the other side, stripped down to the barest part of who he was. That night, Jacob had a strange experience with a "man" whom Jacob later identified as God:

> So Jacob was left alone, and a man wrestled with him till daybreak. When the man saw that he could not overpower him, he touched the socket of Jacob's hip so that his hip was wrenched as he wrestled with the man (Genesis 32:24-25).

Like Jacob, I have come to a turning point where I know I can't control my circumstances. I am learning that I can't manipulate my way into getting God's promise. What I can do, though, is to try to find God in the midst of my circumstances. God has come to wrestle with me. And after all these years I have learned this: I would rather wrestle with God than try to control my circumstances and be called "the one who wants to be what she is not."

I want to see the real God, not some version I create of him that suits all my needs. As C.S. Lewis wrote while reflecting on the death of his wife, "My idea of God is not a divine idea. It has to be shattered time after time. He shatters it himself. He is the great iconoclast. Could we not say that this shattering is one of the marks of his presence?"[5]

I want to wrestle with God like Jacob did. I want to ask him the hard questions, not necessarily to get the answers I want, but to understand him more. I want us to look at each other face-to-face and to be brutally honest, not for the sake of being right but for the sake of being intimate.

Because he is the great iconoclast, the one who shatters false idols, he might shatter my image of him. When I wrestle him, he will be more mind-boggling and infinitely bigger than the box I have put him in. I have contorted him like a street performer to fit him into a little box. But that box must break down. Then perhaps I will accept him for all that he is, even the parts I don't understand. He will transform the way I see him, and, thus, he will transform the way I see myself.

Jacob's story goes on:

> Then the man said, "Let me go, for it is daybreak."
>
> But Jacob replied, "I will not let you go unless you bless me."
>
> The man asked him, "What is your name?"
>
> "Jacob," he answered.
>
> Then the man said, "Your name will no longer be Jacob, but Israel, because you have struggled with God and with men and have overcome."
>
> Jacob called the place Peniel* saying, "It is because I saw God face to face, and yet my life was spared" (Genesis 32:26-30).

At the end of their wrestling, Jacob asked for a blessing. God could have offered Jacob many things for this blessing—more wealth, more fame, more wives. But God offered none of these

---

* Peniel means "Face of God."

things because he knew there was one thing that Jacob wanted more than anything else, and that was what God wanted to give him.

He offered Jacob a new name.

Jacob took that offer gladly. After being called "deceiver" every day of his life, he was ready for a new identity.

God changed Jacob's name to *Israel*. Israel means "one who wrestles with God." God said he gave him this name because Jacob "struggled with God and man and overcame" (Genesis 32:28). He was now named "overcomer."

Overcomer became Jacob's new identity. He was no longer *deceiver*. God changed his name, and that changed everything.

Jacob's new name, Israel, was the name that was given as an inheritance to his descendants. It is the name that is still used today for the chosen people, a people that we as the body of Christ have been grafted into. We are no longer called manipulators or supplanters. We are the ones who have wrestled with God and have come out changed. The ones who have met him face to face.

Revelation 2:17 says, "To him who overcomes, I will give...a white stone with a new name written on it, known only by him who receives it."

This verse closely parallels the story of Jacob. A new name will be given to him who overcomes, to him who wrestles. The new name is so intimate; it is something that is only between you and God.

What is the name that God has given you? What is the name that will overcome your insecurities, the lies you have been told? Take a moment and ask God what this new name, this new identity is for you.

I want to wrestle with God, even if is difficult. I want my new name, my new identity. When I wrestle him, he will tell me to ask the hard questions. He might not give me the answers I want. He might not give me any answers.

But it is his choice. He is God.

In the end I know that I want a God who is free, not a God who answers as if prayers are spells I can cast on my life by saying the right words. I don't want a God like the millions of trinket-gods on street corners around the world who can be bribed with offerings. I want a God who is bigger than me, who is stronger than me, and who comes down and wrestles with me so that we can be close.

And after my wrestling, I may walk away with a limp, like Jacob. But receiving a limp is better than pushing God away. For in my wrestling, I touch God. I touch the God who speaks a word, and stars and moon and universe are made. I touch the God who opens his heart and all things tender and all things passionate and all things beautiful flow out like water. That is the God I wrestle with. He and I will touch and sometimes it will hurt, but I will come away changed. I will not leave with the answers to all my questions, but I will have seen the face of God. And I will see love in his eyes.

Maybe my name will be changed like Jacob's was. Maybe I will no longer simply name myself "single," because I will have seen his eyes and I will know the truth:

I am named Beloved.

What names do you give yourself? What names do other people give you? Divorced? Poor? Abandoned? Sick? Widowed? Fatherless? Failure?

Not anymore. Wrestle with your God and know the truth. You are his beloved.

Kate's Corner of Wisdom
How to Communicate

1. Show up.
2. Tell your truth.
3. Trust God.
4. Let go of the outcome.

What Singles Wish Married People Knew

My child,

I watched you as you were sleeping last night. I spilled moonlight over you and kissed your cheek.

I saw that you were crying. You were crying out for that one you have always longed for. The one that I have created you for.

Oh precious one, I tell you this: When you can trust me completely, when you can let go of your dreams of a spouse and give your desires to me, that's when I will bring you the love of your life.

I am forever yours,

Jesus

I remember reading a letter like this as a handout in my Christian campus group when I was in college. It was a very popular letter back then.

The font: calligraphy that looked like real handwriting.

The sentiment in the room: tender.

The result: letter hung from thumbtacks on the walls of thousands of dorm rooms.

The bad theology, bad sermons, and bad books created around this letter: total crap.

I assure you, many a Christian female read that letter, grabbed their Bibles and journals, went to a quiet place, turned their sweet young faces toward heaven with tears in their eyes, and said, "Lord, I let go. I give my husband to you."

Do you know why? Because those women wanted a husband, and, according to the letter, if you want a husband you let go of him first. So they let go of him in order to get him.

Quite ironic, isn't it?

Some of those lovely young coeds got older and didn't get married, not even after many tearful sessions of letting go. Gradually, their prayers went from a serene, quiet, "I let go" to, "Do you hear me, God?! I let go! I let go! I let go!" with their fists pumping the air.

Doesn't really sound like a peaceful place, does it? Then again, David doesn't sound very peaceful when he says, "How long, O LORD? Will you forget me forever? How long will you hide your face from me?" (Psalm 13:1). David too struggled with frustration and longing. He says he watered his pillow with tears (Psalm 6:6).

Of course, David didn't only mourn. There were times that he wildly praised God with everything in him too.

Then again, so do we.

Sometimes we wake up thankful to God. We trust him. We see the way he has provided for us and the way he makes sense out of a life that doesn't often make sense. We recognize some of the freedom we have as singles and some of the benefits, and we are grateful. We worship with all that we are.

Other times, we hear the nineteenth person that week say, "When you least expect to find your spouse, he will come right around the corner."

We suppress the urge to respond, "I definitely gave up expecting it now that I'm over thirty. That formula of yours doesn't seem to be working because I've been 'least expecting it' for over a decade, and it still ain't happenin', sista."

Married friends, I want you to know that sometimes we go home after those conversations and weep and gnash our teeth and water our pillows with tears.

Well, maybe it's not that bad, but it's not very fun.

If I mention the topic of this book to single people, I often hear a multitude of frustrations about what well-meaning married people say to them. By far the most common is some version of that same popular formula:

When you let go, Jesus will bring your spouse.

In fact, this particular equation—the when-you-let-go-your-husband-will-come equation—has been the most popular how-to-not-be-single formula in the church for quite a while. It feels like people are saying, "This isn't out of your control! It's something you just bring to the Lord and then everything will be all right. Don't worry, honey. You just get out there and give it to God and your spouse will come." Ugh.

Married couples, church-at-large, I will let you know a secret right now. Almost every thinking person feels offended and hurt when given this little formula. Because life doesn't work that way. God makes all things right eventually, but not often in our timing or in ways that we expect. And most of the time we can't control our circumstances with simple formulas. There are actually very few things in the Bible that are that formulaic. Certain things are black and white, such as the goodness of God and the mandate to worship. But when it comes to characters in the Bible and their stories— well, they are all different. Everyone's journey is unique and has its own challenges and joys.

Before I sound too cynical, I want to give some credit to all the beautiful, caring, married friends out there. My friend Becca mentioned the other day that a lot of married people have a formula mentality because they actually want to help single people. Humans want a nice, neat, black-and-white answer. We don't like things that don't make sense, especially when it comes to people we love. So if someone is single and really struggling, his or her married friends, pastors, and even other single people often hand out formulas like raffle tickets, hoping to help ease the pain.

I know Becca's right. Married people are not trying to be malicious when they offer the formula; they are trying to be comforting.

But, my friends, it's not comforting. It hurts.

We singles really do want to be comforted, but the formula method often comes across as a "just add water" kind of comfort.

Let me give you a little story to illustrate: Picture me at thirty, eating lunch with Emily. She is someone I love and respect, and she had become a mentor for me at the time of our lunch date. Keep in mind that she got married at twenty-four. (Which, she often points out, felt like a lifetime to her because she had been wanting marriage since she was sixteen. That's eight long years of waiting, she says.) Anyway, at our lunch we talk about dating. I express my frustrations about being single. I am vulnerable enough to tell her that even though I'm trying to trust God, I am really struggling with being alone.

She twirls her angel hair pasta and says, "Kate, do you remember our babysitter, Joann? Well, she also went through a season of really struggling with being single. She cried and battled and finally brought her burden to the Lord. She was able to give up her husband, just like Abraham gave up Isaac. Two weeks later, she met her husband, and he looks just like Ryan Gosling."

"Emily, I am really happy for Joann," I answer. "But she is twenty freaking years old."

"So? What does that have to do with anything?"

Now, in that season of my life, I didn't often stand up to leaders even if I was frustrated. But it was just too much for me this time.

I continue: "I have had a decade more than her of wrestling with God over this issue. Another decade of waking up alone. Another decade of longing for someone to hold me. In all my wrestling, I have had several seasons where I have been content as a single person, embracing the thought of God as my husband. But often those seasons fade and then I'm struggling again. I don't think God laughs at my cycles of frustration. I think he understands. I think he wants to meet me in them."

Emily keeps arguing with me, saying that I just need to "let go" and insinuating that my singleness is my own fault.

I finally say, "Em, please understand me here. If you had a friend who was having multiple miscarriages or had been struggling with barrenness for ten years, would you say to her 'Well, if you just trusted the Lord more with your barrenness, he would give you a baby'? You would never say that! You would recognize how much she mourns the loss, and you would be sensitive in your words. You wouldn't want to hurt her more by saying her struggle was her own fault. At times I feel barren—not only barren as a mother, but barren as a lover, as well. Please, please be sensitive to this barrenness in me. Please don't tell me that I have done something wrong and that the result of my shortcoming is barrenness."

The sad thing is, Emily still didn't get it. She held on to her perception that if I were more consistent in trusting God, he would bring me my man. She had to have another conversation with a single friend of mine before she realized that maybe it wasn't the most sensitive thing in the world to say. She later apologized.

The reason the if-you-just-let-go formula is so frustrating is that it makes us feel like our being single has nothing to do with God's will or our choices or the enemy or any other theory one might have about why difficult things happen. It makes us feel like our singleness is a result of our lack.

We already struggle with feeling like we are lacking when we wonder why we haven't been chosen. Please don't cut that wound deeper.

The formula also makes us feel like our not being married has to do with our relationship with the Lord, which, according to the formula, is also lacking. For most of us singles, our relationship with the Lord is the most sacred relationship we have. Please, please don't criticize that relationship, as well. Don't tear down one of the only relationships in which we feel loved and accepted. Even if you mean well...well, just don't do it.

There is a very thick book of popular maxims and theologies that are not actually in the Bible (though many people might think they are). I like to call this book First Assumptions. It includes verses like, "This too shall pass," "Cleanliness is next to godliness," "God moves in mysterious ways," and "God helps those who help themselves." This book also includes a chapter of formulas, and in it one can find this lovely formula that may very well have come straight from the letter at the beginning of this chapter:

Not letting go = singleness. Letting go = marriage.

Here is Emily's contribution to that chapter:

Relinquishing your dreams to the Lord = husband who looks like Ryan Gosling.

Let's explore some other formulas that might be found in that chapter, shall we?

My friend Jess is a very beautiful blonde girl who has been a missionary in Italy for ten years and is the same age as I am. One day an Italian woman, let's call her Mamma Carmen, came up to her with a little charm necklace that had a picture of a saint on it.

"What's this?" asked Jess.

(Cue accent of Italian mama who doesn't speak much English.) "A necklace for-a you. A picture of-a Saint Anthony."

"Who is Saint Anthony?"

"Is-a the patron saint of-a lost-a things."

"And what have I lost, Mamma Carmen?"

"Oh-a, you know, sweetie."

"No, I don't know. What is that I have lost?"

"You lost-a your husband."

"Mamma Carmen, isn't Saint Anthony usually the saint you pray to for a lost sock or car keys—things like that?"

"Yes, but not-a for you. For you, pray to him for husband. More important than sock."

Mamma Carmen's formula:

Lost husband + praying to Patron Saint of Lost Things + ten Hail Marys = one wedding, five socks, two spoons, and a bracelet you thought you gave to your friend Jill.

It seems to me that the if-you-just-let-go-your-spouse-will-come formula is much more prevalent in church culture than it is in secular culture. In fact, just the other day I was talking to two single guy friends of mine who are both over thirty. One is very involved in church culture and the other doesn't often go to church. I was telling them how hard it was when people give me "the formula," and my non-church-going friend said, "Wait. You guys have had that said to you?"

"Of course," said my other guy friend, "like every week of my life."

"No one has ever said that to me," my unchurched friend said.

It makes you wonder how many of these formulas come from our church culture and not from the Lord's heart.

When used in the wrong context, these pat answers can be very damaging. Donald Miller said, "As much as we want to believe we can fix our lives in about as many steps as it takes to make a peanut butter sandwich, I don't believe we can."[1]

Another example that parallels the experience of singles: When I was sick, I developed a new respect for people who are chronically ill. Sickness like that is difficult beyond words. My illness was on my mind almost every minute of the day. It took so much for me to get past my pain and the wall of exhaustion that I had difficulty keeping my mind on anything else. Of course, my well-meaning friends and other people at church wanted to comfort me.

On one hand, I appreciated how often people prayed for my healing. On the other hand, their "comfort" often came with a note that characters in the Bible were healed because of their faith. This, of course, communicated to me that if I wasn't getting better, it must have been because I didn't have enough faith. According to this formula, my sickness wasn't going away because I was doing something wrong.

I now see that it took a whole lot of faith to get through that sickness still believing that God is good.

It also took a whole lot of faith for my friend Carrie, who battled cancer with incredible composure, to believe in God's goodness. She was healed for a season, praised God, and soon, she got much worse. She died. Does her death mean she didn't have enough faith?

The eulogist at Carrie's funeral was a coworker who was also an atheist. He said that he had never met anyone who loved God like Carrie did. He said that even when her body dwindled away and was ravaged by disease, her face would light up when she talked about Jesus. She was not bitter toward God. Instead, she knew God was her hope. At the end of his speech he said, "I know Carrie is in the arms of Jesus somewhere now, so grateful to finally be with him." This was from an atheist. Everyone in the room was crying.

Carrie praising Jesus on her death bed is just as beautiful a story as someone receiving a miraculous healing. Dying in Christ and living in Christ both take an enormous amount of faith and courage. But we question the person in the deathbed scene because we don't understand it. Sometimes bad things happen and there is no formula or pat answer to explain why they do. It would be wise for us to see the person in the middle of circumstances that we can't understand with compassion, recognizing their strength rather than judging and questioning why they are in those circumstances.

You probably know the story of Job. God and the devil make a bet. The devil says Job will turn away from God if he suffers; God says he'll stay faithful. So Job gets pummeled by dying kids and a ruined house and horrible boils. His wife gets incredibly angry with him. His friends come in and tell him their theories about why he is suffering. They give him all kinds of formulas. Most of the formulas have to do with how Job must have had some hidden sin or was doing something wrong.

Here is the formula we could come up with from Job's story:

> tragically losing everything
> + angry wife
> + hideous boils all over your body
> + friends saying you must have done something to deserve this
> + being totally frustrated and not understanding
> + God saying you don't know as much as you think you do
> + praising God even through horrible circumstances and singing "Blessed Be Your Name"
> _____
> = twice as much stuff as you had before

Formulas do not explain away difficult circumstances.

On top of creating formulas that we think are biblical, we tend to create our own formulas based on our experiences. It is easy to sum up our experiences into pat stories that make everyone else feel like relationships and marriage should look a certain way. Through these new made-up formulas, we tell each other why a relationship does or doesn't, or should or shouldn't, happen.

An example:

My husband and I met in the grocery store aisle, so go put on your cutest sundress, grab some strawberries, and then nonchalantly drop the strawberries in front of that cute guy in the produce section.

Or if a single person has gone through a bad breakup, a married person will often use their own experience as a formula to make the unmarried person feel like it might still work out.

We had been broken up for two years. I was on a date with someone else, and he came in with an engagement ring and said that he realized he couldn't live without me. We've been married eight years now.

The motivation of the married person here is not to give false hope. He or she just wants to make an uncontrollable situation seem more controllable. But you know what? These formulas often do give us false hope.

If a married (or divorced) person has gone through something really hard, he or she will often make a formula out of that experience as well. I have heard both of these:

Don't ever ever ever marry your best friend. It will never work out.
and
Don't ever ever ever marry someone who is not your best friend. It will never work out.

Married people, pastors, ministry leaders, you need to realize that when single people are in a season of loneliness, we often cling to the formulas you give us. We will put makeup on to go to the grocery store to get strawberries and drop them like they're hot because someone once said that is a good way to get husbands.

When there has been a breakup, our instinct to cling to formulas gets even stronger…and can be even more detrimental. The story about the proposal from the guy two years after the couple broke up? I have thought of that story many times after my own breakups, and it has given me false hope.

It's not that I don't want to hear your story. I love hearing people's stories. Sometimes the stories have helped. But other times, when your story turns into a black-and-white formula, the advice can become unhealthy. If I cling to that breakup story when I am lonely and I want my boyfriend back, I need to step back and take caution. Every story is different, and both married people and singles need to remember that.

I think a good rule of thumb is to do less formula making and pat-answering and to do more listening. Listening and loving are so closely related that sometimes it's hard to tell the difference. Listen to what the Lord has to say and listen to what the one who is struggling has to say. We singles might ask you for formulas—even beg you for formulas—because we want you to be able to help us fix things. But for the most part, those formulas don't help.

I don't want to make it sound like you shouldn't feel free to share your own experience as a married person, but I also want to make it very clear that everyone's journey is different. Try not to let your own emotions, your own hopes, and your own frustrations go into your advice-giving. Try to restrain yourself from giving out formulas.

But never restrain yourself from giving us a hug. We probably really need one.

And singles, maybe we should stop clinging to formulas like dryer sheets cling to clothes. Maybe we need to realize that we have our own journeys, and all of our journeys are valid.

What Married People Wish Singles Knew

My brother, Will, and my sister-in-law, Marie, had twins last October. The twins were 8 pounds 10 ounces and 7 pounds 7 ounces. That's sixteen pounds of baby inside another human being.

Will and Marie also have a beautiful four-year-old with cerebral palsy named John Mark. He is one of the loves of my life. Because John Mark can't walk, they have had three non-walking children for over a year since the birth of the twins. When Will takes the kids out, he straps one twin into a carrier on his front and one on his back, and then he sets John Mark in a stroller. Watching Will cart around three babies is as fascinating to watch as it is to watch a woman in Africa putting forty-eight pounds of water on her head.

The twins are now a year and a half old, and I recently visited their family for Christmas. Will and I put on a puppet show on Christmas morning complete with a spontaneous song called "No Tacos for Christmas" that we performed with Latino accents. The three kids sat on chairs in front of the homemade puppet theatre and belly-laughed for a full hour.

It is during moments like those that I ache for children of my own.

A day or so after the puppet show, we went to the dentist's office. Marie asked me to watch the twins for half an hour while she got her teeth cleaned. I had worked at a daycare for five years, so I didn't think that watching them would be very difficult.

I was wrong.

Jeremiah crawls crazy fast. I think he could beat most Olympians. His speed made my time at the dentist's office difficult, to say the least. When I held Arowyn, Jeremiah crawled down the hallway at record speeds, straight toward the dentist's not-childproofed drills. When I set Arowyn down to grab her brother, she went speeding down the hallway toward that fun buzzing noise, which was actually someone getting a root canal. Surely a root canal is not a procedure during which a dentist would want an adorable toddler underfoot.

I spent those minutes running down the hallway, picking one baby up and plopping it down in the waiting room and then running down the hallway again, picking the other baby up and plopping that one down in the waiting room. This went on for what seemed like forever. Within minutes, I was frazzled. I was perplexed as to how Will and Marie could do this for fourteen hours a day.

Will and Marie barely ever complain about their kids. When asked, they don't go on a tyrannical rampage explaining how having twins is harder than surviving the bubonic plague. (I have heard other people make this analogy about their twins.) In fact, Will and Marie often refer to their children as the most important blessing of their lives. There is power in speaking blessing, even when a child can't understand those words. Will and Marie are also superhumanly patient when their children are screaming louder than a bad emo band for nine hours straight.

I understand that having a family is difficult. After I spend time with Will and Marie and their kids, I realize one important thing:

I. Do. Not. Get. It.

I don't understand what it is like to live day-to-day with someone, with their weaknesses exposed for me to see on a regular basis. I don't understand what it is like to have children vying for my attention every hour of the day, like Will and Marie do. I can't understand it because I haven't experienced it.

Let me add something here. I do struggle with people telling me how hard marriage is, which is the default response when people find out that I am in my thirties and not married. They often feel like it is their duty to warn me of the impending doom that will be mine if I choose matrimony as my life sentence.

I usually get defensive when this happens, thinking, "My life can be hard too! I would give up a lot to have someone choose me. To have children." But lately, after seeing more and more friends divorce, I have been thinking it might be wiser for me to listen than to get angry. The truth is, people like Will and Marie have experience that I don't have. I should discipline the bratty children named Ego and Arrogance inside my head. I should take to heart the advice of my married friends and learn something that will help me love better whether I get married or not. Thus, I have decided to interview several couples and several divorced people for this book, and I have asked them to share their advice for us single people.

"Oh no!" I'm sure you are yelling right about now. "I trusted you, Kate. Yours is the first book I have read in a long time that has not told me in the first few sentences that I am required to appreciate my gift of singleness. How could you make me sit through married-people advice?"

Calm yourself. The following points were said so many times by the people I interviewed that I think they are worth listening to. Paying attention here could save us many years of heartache, and it could greatly benefit the relationships we have now too.

Take a deep breath. Let's walk through this together. We will be all right. And it will be worth it. Here is the advice that was mentioned the most by my interviewees.

Get as healthy as possible while you are single.

During your single years, your dysfunction mostly affects you and your own life. When you are married, your dysfunction deeply affects the closest people in your lives and can potentially hurt them. My spiritual mom told me this years ago, and her advice was one of the reasons I started seeing a counselor. I wanted to be a healthier person, both to honor myself and to honor the family I may have one day.

Some people think that only crazies get counseling. But I have come to believe that people who invest in their own emotional well-being are the healthiest people I know because they actually work to get better. A person who has a huge splinter of wood buried in them is not healthy. They might seem fine, but there is probably an infection under the surface. A person who wants to be healthy realizes that they have some issues and goes to a professional to get that splinter of wood removed.

I am a frugal person, but I have learned that my emotional and physical health are two things I shouldn't scrimp on. Professional help is invaluable if you want to live a better life. Spending money on counseling is, hands down, the best money I have ever spent.

It is important to look for an amazing person that we want to spend the rest of our lives with, but it is just as important to become an amazing person. Working on our emotional well-being through counseling is an important way to do this. Furthermore, if we work on our emotional well-being, we will attract a person who is at the same level of health we are. The healthier we are, the more likely we are to attract someone who is also healthy. But let's not work on ourselves just to attract people. Let's work on ourselves because we deserve to be healthy.

Truly, being emotionally stable is way more fun than being a basket case. Take it from me. I've been both.

In addition to going to counseling as a single person, I think we'd be wise to also consider going to counseling once we start seriously dating someone. Although it sounds foreign to go to "dater's counseling," doing so makes sense. Either the counseling will help a couple see that they are not a good match or it will help build a good foundation for the future marriage. Worth every penny.

Be careful with your expectations of marriage.

Re-read the chapter on expectations. Then re-read it again. Then ponder if re-reading what you re-read means that you re-re-read it. Then be reminded of this important point: You will save yourself immeasurable amounts of disappointment if you have realistic expectations about marriage. This was the advice most emphasized to me by my married friends.

As I mentioned in the previous chapter, if your expectations are too high going into a marriage, you can end up resenting the person you marry simply because they are not fulfilling you the way you wanted them to.

The more we keep our expectations in check now, the easier it will be for us to keep our expectations in check when we are married. If we can foresee that false expectations are a dangerous road to go down, we will not put as much pressure on our spouse to give us happiness if we do get married. Remember that unrealistic expectations can often become premeditated resentments.

Recognize how weighty the decision to marry is.

Decide with both your heart and your head whether or not it is a wise choice to marry the person you are dating. Deciding whom we marry is probably the most important decision of our lives. It will affect everything. Both married and divorced people I interviewed stressed this point again and again, especially if they made hasty decisions that they regretted later.

Turns out, most people don't have the best judgment when first in love. There is a good reason for this: Most of them are basically thinking like drug addicts. Seriously. According to the National Public Radio show *Radiolab*, in an episode called, "This Is Your

Brain on Love," scientists have looked at the brains of people who are newly in love and compared them to the brains of cocaine addicts. They looked very similar.

When we fall in love, we become addicted to a number of naturally occurring chemicals. The most prominent one is dopamine. This is a chemical that makes a person feel happy and passionate. When first attracted to someone, a person has huge surges of dopamine running through his or her body.

If dopamine were a woman at a party she would be the one who is a really good kisser and looks amazing in her skin-tight outfit but really doesn't want anything long-term. She comes on strong and it feels really good to be around her, but her commitment quickly fades. Her love is not the kind of love that is sustainable.

Thankfully, after six months or so of being in a relationship with someone, a hormone called oxytocin comes into the mix that starts displacing the dopamine. This chemical is marked with a sense of calm and stability rather than with unsustainable highs. It lasts much longer than dopamine, even if it doesn't make a person as "happy." It helps one person attach to another, and it promotes contentment in that relationship.

Oxytocin is comparable to that really nice girl next door with a southern accent. The one who is not as flashy but who has a good heart and who would probably make a really good wife someday.[1]

Our Hollywood-saturated society often gives us the idea that love is simply having the feeling that dopamine gives us. But chemicals that make us uncontrollably passionate are not what make love last. They may help draw us to someone, but they don't foster long-term commitment. Once we are committed to our mate, dopamine will help bring a little romance, but it is not the glue that holds a marriage together. It is sobering to see how many divorces and affairs have happened because people have mistaken this chemically induced feeling for love and have abandoned their partner when the "love" wears off.

Interesting, isn't it? Perhaps we should keep this theory in mind as we date. Perhaps we should remember that our brains are bowls of hormonal soup right now. And bowls of hormonal soup do not often make good decisions.

Let's let ourselves be in love. Let's be aware and appreciative of this special season during which it feels so good to be in someone's presence. Let's let dopamine do its job and let it attract us to someone who could be a good partner. But let's not put dopamine in the driver's seat and let it propel us to make big decisions unwisely.

Clearly, we will need to give ourselves time while we are dating to let some of these chemicals wear off so we can be sober in our decision-making. Romance and the feeling of being high on love won't guarantee a good marriage. Rather than relying solely on our feelings to make decisions, we should be sure to ask lots of practical questions over time about the person we are dating. *Does this person have a good track record in how he or she has treated me? Do I keep telling myself that he has good potential? That she will get better with time?* Getting married to someone who has a good track record is a pretty safe choice. Marrying someone who just has potential is not very safe. And track records take time.

There is great wisdom in looking for the fruit of something even when it is still a seed. Yes, you might be in love now, but what will it be like to have children with this person? What will it be like to grow old with him or her? Maybe his obsession with Super Mario Brothers is cute now, but will it be cute in ten years if he is lazy and doesn't want to work? Maybe you are able to excuse her road rage now, but will her anger find its way to you or your children in the future?

Our married friends are right: We need to realize what a big decision it is to marry someone and take practical steps towards making that decision with clearheaded wisdom.

Let's remember to invite discernment on our dates and wisdom to the wedding.

(Oh my gosh, I just saw my future. It involved me saying that phrase with a puppet on my hand on a Christian cable show called "Kate's Corner o' Dating Wisdom." Should I be scared, or should I get plastic surgery?)

Wait to get engaged until the removal of the projections happens.

Some of the best advice I ever heard about dating came from my brilliant counselor. She says that every couple goes through what she calls the "removal of the projections." According to her, when you start to date someone, you project the very best version of yourself toward him or her. (Think eHarmony profile here.) You also project your own version of the perfect person onto the one you are with. You see them as perfect when they really aren't. When you are first in love, it's easy to overlook or ignore weaknesses.

But when the removal of the projections happens, the projections on both sides come down and you see and are seen as you really are, weaknesses and all. When this happens, both parties often try to control the other because both are desperately wanting to keep the projection going and to believe that the other is perfect. Both parties also want to maintain the belief that they themselves are perfect too. At that point, according to my counselor, there either comes a point of acceptance or a point of separation. Of course, this cycle can happen several times in the course of a relationship.

From my counselor's experience, it is much healthier to have the removal of the projections happen while a couple is dating rather than after the pair gets married. If it happens while dating, there is great security in knowing that your potential partner wants to be with you even if you are not perfect. Alternatively, the removal of the projections can be a mirror that will help you break up if you realize that you aren't a good fit and that a marriage with this person would be extremely difficult.

If the removal of the projections happens after marriage, however, you can feel trapped. Of course, if you are married you can choose to love the person regardless of what arises, but it makes sense to me that it would be a good goal to have enough time and experience to let at least the initial removal of the projections happen while dating.

Explore what it means to be in covenant, even before you are in one.

This point closely relates to having the right expectations about marriage. This is not Hollywood, people, it is covenant. Covenant is hard work, and it is beautiful work.

Danny Silk provides a good definition of covenant as a "binding agreement that requires death."[2]

In Genesis 15, after God tells Abraham that his descendants would outnumber the stars, he seals this covenant by having Abraham sacrifice several animals. This was the first covenant that God made with Abraham, and it required death.

Throughout the Old Testament, we see a lot more covenant requiring a lot more death. God regularly commands an animal sacrifice to be made in the outer courts in order for the priest to go into the Holy of Holies and speak with him. And what was the name of the place where God dwelled? The Ark of the *Covenant*.

Most importantly, in the most stunning act of commitment in history, Jesus came to die so that our covenant with him would be sealed.

A definition of marriage that includes the word *death* is a lot harder to swallow than a definition that includes lots of roses, sex all the time, and the ability to use all of those two-for-one coupons we've saved for ten years. It is important for us to prepare for the beautiful difficulty that is waiting for us on the other side of covenant. When we say *yes* to our potential spouse, we are saying yes to serving and sacrificing in ways that we never understood before.

My friend Brandon said to me the other day that there is a difference between contract and covenant. A contract, by definition, he said, involves an agreement that stands as long as each party lives up to their side of the bargain. Covenant, however, says, "You are family to me. Even if there are times when you don't live up to your part of the bargain, you are still my family."

If you are holding on to someone for reasons other than wanting to bring beautiful things to his or her life, you should examine your motivation. There have certainly been times when I stayed with a boyfriend not because we were a good match and because we would bless each other's lives, but because I really wanted to be married. (This is not a good reason to stay together.)

Conversely, if you get the feeling your potential spouse is marrying you just so they will feel like they are valuable or because they like your 1976 El Camino, I beg you…run away fast!

But if you are in this thing to better each other's lives…well, that can grow into something beautiful.

As a group of philosophers that went by the name DC Talk said many years ago, "Love is a verb." Love is not just about feeling good; it's about a choice to commit.

Realize that love is not only about taking a bullet for someone, but it is also about taking out the trash.

The InnerChange base I lived on had a great sign hanging over the kitchen sink. It said, "Everyone wants to start a revolution, but nobody wants to do the dishes." That sign guilted a lot of revolutionary, social-justice-hipster-Christians to buckle down and get that crusty cheese off of their bowl.

This sign makes a good point: Big sacrifices are sometimes easier to make than small sacrifices. We all think that we would do something noble for someone we love, like throw our bodies over them while a double agent from Belarus tries to shoot them with a semi-automatic. The truth is, the double-agent-to-normal-citizen ratio is very low. Odds are we will never have to do anything like that.

However, if we have children, odds are we will have to wake up in the middle of the night to calm down a screaming baby about 835 times. I promise you, men, that if you get up and do that, you will be more of a hero to your sleep-deprived wife than you would be if you ran in front of a train to rescue her favorite Gucci bag.

As we think about our future and present families, we'd do well to listen to this advice: If you want to love your family well, commit to doing thoughtful and uncomfortable things on a daily basis. Taking out the trash may not seem valiant, but when you do it to show respect and love for your family, it adds up to an important sacrifice.

The definition of *heroic* may be to take a bullet for someone, but integrity is about making small choices every day that bring honor to the people you love. That is something to remember whether we are married or not.

Learn to communicate.

This nugget of advice is a big one for me. When I was growing up, the only time I can remember having a family meeting was when my parents told us they were getting a divorce. In my family, confrontation often meant harsh arguing. When there wasn't arguing, there was silence. In my mind, confrontation equaled trauma. No wonder I grew up terrified of communicating. No wonder I have to work through my feelings of being terrified of communicating now.

No problem, though. All I have to do is stuff my feelings down and never talk about them, right? Well, if I want unhealthy relationships forever, I can stick with that plan. But I love people. I want to connect. And the only way that I can connect is to communicate.

After working through a lot of these issues the last few years, I have gotten much better at communicating. It has changed my life.

If you haven't looked at "How to Communicate" on page 96, check it out. Learning these four simple steps will help you walk the road toward communicating well.

I'll recap. First, show up. Showing up simply means to choose not to hide from conflict and to make space for communication to happen. Remember that the more you hide what is going on inside of you, the less alive you are. Second, tell your truth. In order to tell your truth, you have to take good inventory of what is going on inside you. Figure out what you are feeling and speak it out. Don't tell someone what you think they want to hear; tell them the truth that is going on inside you. Third, trust God. And fourth, let go of the outcome. This means that you realize you can never control someone's response to what you say, and you can't control what happens after you say it. All you can control is what you say and how you respond.

Even though these steps are a good guideline for communicating well, there is so much more to learn about communication and lots of good resources to help us. I think it would be very wise of us to follow the advice of our married friends by committing to read books and listen to teachings on communication even before we are married.

If our goal is to love well, there is nothing more important than to work on being a good communicator.

Learn your partner's code book.

In Dann Farrelly's teaching "Brave Communication," which is the best and most practical teaching on communication that I have ever heard, he talks about how every person has what he calls a "code book" that contains the person's perspective on life. Parents, classmates, teachers, past girlfriends or boyfriends, habits developed as children, and cultural expectations all contribute to this book. By the time a person is an adult, this book is as thick as a phone book and is very, very complicated. When two people's code books come together, those unique perspectives can be difficult to unite and may cause a lot of miscommunication.

Here is a good example of the clash of the code books: I had a boyfriend once who, every time we got off the phone, said, "See ya."

I hated it. I hated it when we first started dating, and I hated it even more after we were dating for a year.

Being a typical idealistic girl, I wanted him to end our conversations saying, "You are the most beautiful woman on earth. In fact, you are more like a goddess than a mere woman. Your absence is like a thread that weaves through the very fiber of my being. So for now, farewell, my love. I wait for the moment I see you again, for that is the moment I will come back to life."

Instead, I got "See ya."

My default stance was to take his way of saying goodbye as a sign that he didn't love me. But I came to realize that there was more to it than that: It was more of a codebook issue than a love issue. I started noticing that every person in his family also ended conversations with the same nonchalance. Eventually, I realized that in my code book, "See ya" was a flippant thing said to an acquaintance, and it made me feel devalued. But in his code book, it was the equivalent of saying "goodnight" or "goodbye." Understanding his code book helped us relate to each other with more understanding and love.

We should be aware when something our partner does that frustrates us is truly an issue with sin and when it is simply an issue with his or her code book. An important part of being in a relationship is learning to love the other person enough to start reading through their code book and be compassionate toward their perspective and journey.[3]

Marriage is like driving.

When my friend Halen was about to get married, we all gave her marriage advice at her bachelorette party. As you can tell from this book, I am the queen of giving advice about things that I don't have much experience with. Romantic relationships, for example. But the advice that came out of my mouth that night made a lot of sense, and I'm going to pass it on to you. Therefore, this particular point of the chapter is not coming from a married person, but it is still worth listening to.

This is what I told her: Dating and marriage might seem pretty terrifying. In fact, life is sort of a crapshoot. It's all so risky! How could you possibly foresee and prepare for the problems you might have? Comparing relationships to driving will take some of the fear out of the equation. What if I was so scared of driving that I never left home? What if I said, "I can't do this whole traveling thing! A blue-haired lady might come out of nowhere and try to get in my lane! A biker might ride dangerously close to me! I might get both of my hands tied up while I'm taking my coat off! That's it. I'm staying home."

It is risky to drive, I told Halen. We can't possibly foresee the problems that will come before we are actually on the road. So we have to get in the car and take the problems as we go, overcoming them one by one. We see a yellow light and we slow down. We see a biker and we get out of the way. We see a blue-haired lady and we pass her so we do not have to endure 35 mph commutes.

What I'm saying is, yes, knowing the rules of the road could save us from getting into a bad accident. Yes, it would be wise to look at a map if we don't know where we are going. But worrying about problems you cannot foresee will stop you from ever taking any risks. And a life without risks is no life at all.

Your job is not to avoid risk and stay home. Your job is to get in the car and do the next right thing. Sometimes the next right thing is to overcome fear and commit to someone. And even after that, all you have to do is the next right thing.

Doesn't that make all of this dating and marrying stuff a little less scary? It does for me.

Remember, there are never perfect matches, but there are good matches.

According to my married friends, it is impossible to find the perfect person to be with. There are no perfect people. Every person on earth is going to have some things you like about them and some things you don't like.

I'm sure you're familiar with the idea of "the one." This idea says that there is one and only one person who is your soul mate. No one else out there is right for you, so you better look hard for them. Most married people I talked to no longer believe in this concept. In fact, divorced friends of mine have told me they think that believing in "the one" can hurt marriages. According to them, when a marriage gets difficult it is easy to think, *Oh no! Maybe this is not the one! Maybe I should leave this person so I can find the one!*

I personally believe that two people never start out as soul mates, but they grow into soul mates over time. It is less helpful to ask yourself if a potential mate is *the one* and more helpful to ask if they are a good match or a bad match.

Let me give you an example in my own life of a bad match. I was with a man for a long time who was very different from me. He was very logical and analytical. We would sort through issues for hours at a time. We tried really hard to come to agreements with each other. He loved to discuss things. Now, I like discussing things, but I also really like to have fun. I felt like I was losing my sense of humor and he didn't feel like he could be as analytical as he wanted to be.

After a while, it was clear that our issues were not merely code book issues. We were just not a good match for each other. I beat myself up, thinking I had done something wrong or that I had been someone wrong. But the truth was, we would probably have had a really hard time if we had gotten married, even if we really loved each other.

It was not our fault. We were just not a good match. Some people's personalities simply go together better. There is no rhyme or reason to this. Chemistry is a real thing, and so is compatibility.

How can you tell if the person you are dating is a bad match for you? First, you need to ask yourself if you can handle the hard things times ten. If you get married, you will probably have to deal with them times ten. You also need to weigh their good qualities against the bad, deciding if the good is worth the bad. These are all things you can only learn with good information as you date someone.

Again, take inventory to decide if you are jumping to the conclusion that you are not a good match just because you are scared to commit. If you have given it time and have gotten good information about one another and it still feels like trying to hammer a round peg into a square hole, however, do not beat yourself up. It may simply be that you are just not compatible.

Go on a road trip to Coney Island.

I am a traveller. I refuse to believe that I will never do anything adventurous again after I have a family. I have seen people travel with families. In fact, my dear friend's baby has been to more countries than I have, and he's only one year old. He has been to ten countries and twenty states! Getting married does not have to mean that all things fun in life cease to exist. I might have to make a conscious decision to get out the door with my family and go camping rather than obsessing over the stain that won't come out of the kitchen floor, but I can do it.

Despite this, married people have suggested that I come to grips with the fact that my life will be drastically different if I get married and have children.

I know, I know. We singles hate it when marrieds tell us that we should do everything we can while we are single because we have loads of extra time. We often think we've had enough adventures and just want to have babies.

We also wonder why our married friends say stuff like that. I don't feel like I have lots of time! But I guess, really, I do have more time than most of my married friends because I can usually make boundaries and say no to things in order to have more time. They can't. When little Tommy is wiping his diaper on the wall, for example, you really can't say no to that. You have to deal with it.

I will let you in on a little secret. I expect that our married friends tell us that we should have lots of adventures before we are married because they really, honestly, mean it. They miss having more freedom.

Covenant is, by its very nature, constraining. It implies having new, stricter boundaries. In marriage you take the other person's life, preferences, schedule, and a million other things and make them your own. Those things, compiled with having the responsibility of bringing several small human beings into the world and helping them comprehend the meaning of life, along with feeding them strained carrots, can really be a time suck. That is not just something our married friends say to amuse us or make us mad. It is the truth.

Maybe we should get over ourselves, go to Coney Island with our roommates, and thoroughly enjoy ourselves.

Try to be a true helpmate for your partner.

I want to end with this point because it so beautifully sums up what a good relationship should look like.

Two Hebrew words, *ezar* ("power, strength") and *kenegdo* ("who stands opposite and looks in the face"), are translated as *helpmate* in the Old Testament.[4] We often think *helpmate* connotes that one person is under the other. The true essence of the word, however, is that there are two whole people—equals—who are strong for themselves and strong for the other. They stand opposite each other, and, in doing so, they look each other in the face. Their being opposite of each other is not a bad thing; it gives them strength. Because they are opposite, they are able to look behind their beloved to see what their beloved cannot and protect them from it. The more these two communicate with each other, the more they are able to learn from the perspective of the one who stands opposite of them.

This beautifully depicts what we should strive for in any relationship. We are to work toward wholeness, toward being strong in ourselves so we can be strong for each other. We are to be confident in our stance, standing opposite but learning to communicate so that our differences add to the other person's life. We are to look at the person in the face, an act that depicts both vulnerability and intimacy. We are to dance together, a dance in which our opposite natures bring beauty rather than strife.

11

What Divorced People Wish Everybody Knew

My dear friend Roger was first diagnosed with thyroid cancer when he was 18 years old. He suffered through the ordeal three separate times. Through a miraculous turn of events that included the first tumor disappearing after prayer, his friends giving him his own personal prom in his hospital room, his going to Africa despite doctors saying he needed to stay home to get treatment, surviving a horrific car accident, and many more incredible details, he doesn't have cancer any more. He does, however, have a long scar that goes down the length of his neck.

Before I knew Roger's story, that scar looked kind of scary to me. I wondered if he got it in a bar fight or from being mauled by a bear (which, in fact, is what he told me before he shared with me the real details). I didn't know about God's hand in that story because I assumed he did something brave or crazy on his own.

Roger eventually took several hours to tell me his story of healing, and that scar has become one of the most beautiful parts of him to me. It's such an indication of God's mind-blowing faithfulness in his life. That scar is beautiful because it tells his story. It's a mark of God's unfathomable love, and it's also a mark of Roger's strength through his trial and his trust in the goodness of God.

Kisses may be wonderful, but they only last for a moment. Scars are painful, but these marks of your strength overcoming wounds last a lifetime.

I was reminded of Roger's scar last night after talking to a friend who is going through a difficult divorce. As he told me his story, I realized he has a scar just as prominent as Roger's that people see when they look at him. A scar named *divorce*. Without knowing his story, you might think it was ugly. You might think he has it because he is a bad person. But maybe, just like Roger, if you knew his story, you might see that scar differently.

Fred Rogers, the late host of the PBS children's program *Mister Rogers' Neighborhood*, carried a piece of paper with him everywhere that said, "Frankly, there isn't anyone you couldn't learn to love once you've heard their story."[1]

If you have been divorced, like my friend, you have scars—and they are difficult to cover up. Divorce is so personal and so public. Many of the rest of us have scars underneath our clothes, scars other people can't see. We can hide them well. But divorced people are forced to show their scars to the world.

If you have been through a divorce, I am here to honor you and the scar you bear. Like my friend's scar, it marks a painful journey you walked through and survived. Now, please don't misinterpret this—I'm not saying divorce is a good thing. Covenant is important, and we see that truth throughout the Bible. But we can never judge someone who has been through a tragedy like this. We cannot know the dark night of the soul they have been through or why they had to make such a monumentally difficult choice.

I went through the vicious divorce of my parents when I was eleven years old, and the experience was as devastating as you can imagine. Two people tearing themselves apart from each other feels unnatural and horrible because it *is* unnatural and horrible. In the deepest love story, God marries his bride and the marriage is eternal. So it doesn't feel right for earthly marriages to end.

In God's original plan, people would never stop loving each other and would never be ripped from each other like that. We do not live in that original plan. Yes, God hates divorce—Scripture affirms that in Malachi 2:16. But God doesn't hate the people going through a divorce. He loves them so deeply. He cares about every intimate detail of this life-wrenching event.

It seems that the church often judges divorced people, doubting their faith and their integrity. And I do believe divorce should be a last resort, as in cases of abuse and adultery, and not just the default thing to do when life together becomes difficult. But think about this for a moment: How much faith does it take to keep believing in a good God after going through something as horrible as divorce? How much integrity does it take to keep going to church when so much judgment is attached to attendance? How much strength can a person possibly hold after so many tears, so many yearnings, so much desire for things to be different?

While Scripture, as I've noted, is clear that God hates divorce, we can't use those verses to label people who are going through their own personal hell. We don't know their stories. It's neither fair nor helpful to judge those in pain. Instead, we need to recognize that these people have walked into their own personal cave and come out still believing in God's goodness. They have the wisdom that comes only with experience. They understand how to love better a second time. We as a church need to humble ourselves and learn from their experience.

My friend Brandon and his wife, Melissa, looked like the perfect couple. They bought a house and began renovating it—a symbol of the love they were also building with each other. But suddenly, out of the blue, Melissa left.

Dreams were attached to that house. Dreams that involved family and laughter and hope. Even after his wife left and the house was empty, Brandon had invested so much money in it that he was forced to continue renovations. He knew while he was finishing it that someone else—most likely a family—would live there instead of him.

He could have chosen to become bitter. But now, two years later, he has finished renovating that old house. He has decided to move on and build a new home. He loved that old house, but he can't live there anymore. The home he is building now is different from the one he expected to live in. Nevertheless, it's a home that will end up being beautiful.

Brandon says, "There are people in my life who expect me to be angry at Melissa. But we've all lost our way at some point, haven't we? The forest grows over our path, the vines block our way, we become lost in the wilderness, wondering if there is a God in heaven who cares. My wife left me, but I forgive her. She abandoned me, but God has not. My dreams were crushed, but God is rebuilding them. He is using my brokenness to build the kingdom."

Brandon's story illustrates beautifully that when any of us goes through a struggle, we have a choice set before us. Deuteronomy 30:19 says, "I have set before you life and death, blessings and curses. Now choose life, so that you and your children may live." We can choose death, growing angry at people and God and letting our bitterness seep through our very being. Or we can choose life by forgiving deeply and thoroughly.

Forgiveness is key for people going through a divorce. Small, everyday choices—this consistent choosing of life, this forgiveness that keeps on covering—will determine whether scars will fester and be full of infection or be gilded with the gold of true wisdom, of learning to love deeper.

Healing comes from a journey, not a formula. If you are divorced, you are absolutely allowed to grieve. You are absolutely allowed to have moments of deep anger and weeping and confusion. But with the power of forgiveness, you can know that divorce isn't the end of your story.

I interviewed several divorced people for this chapter. Many of them said the hardest part of dating as a divorced person is that potential partners see you as "used goods."

If you are considering dating a divorced person, you need to realize divorce is a difficult mark, but you should not overlook someone just because of that mark. You don't know the heart of that person until you get to know them. You need to take time to understand the journey they have been through. As always, you should be wise in your dating and get to know them over time, but don't give up on them without knowing their heart.

Similarly, we need to give grace to people in our churches who have been divorced. My friend John reflects on the season soon after his divorce:

> I was in a difficult place. It would not have been good for me to be given a strong leadership position. But my friends at church still treated me with respect and gave me simple responsibilities that helped me know I still had a place there. They let me play drums on the worship team, and after a while they asked me to come on a trip with the youth. I stopped drinking before I went on that trip because I was given responsibility, and I wanted to take that responsibility seriously. My friends kept me accountable, but they also made a place for me. People at church often encouraged me and spoke promises of hope over me.
>
> If you refuse to accept someone who is divorced, it's like saying that the blood of Christ does not cover them. The forgiveness that Jesus offers extends to all people, including those who are divorced. Treat them that way.

Now, several years later, John helped start a worship movement called Resound. He speaks and plays all over the world. He believes that people speaking destiny into his life and extending understanding while he was going through his divorce helped to bring him where he is now.

I am going to end this chapter with the story of one of my dear pastors, Brad Reilly. He went to Cambodia to understand the sex trafficking epidemic. What he saw there shook him to the very core. Brad had nightmares for months. He told us from the pulpit that he had even struggled with his pastorship because it was so hard for him to reconcile God's goodness with what he had seen.

But eventually Brad understood something that changed his perspective on what he was going through. He imagined God saying, *Brad, there is a cave of evil that many men refuse to look into. It is too painful. Suffering lives in that cave. War and disease and sex trafficking and orphans and divorce live in that cave. Most people want to ignore that cave and pretend it is not there.*

But what if I have chosen you to walk into that cave? To look at what is inside of it so that you can bring light?

You have three choices in front of you. First, you can ignore that that cave exists. If you do that, nothing in the world will ever change. You can ask, Where is goodness? *without acknowledging that for this season I use you to bring my goodness. Second, you can walk into that cave without me, which will probably result in a sad, bitter life. Third, you can walk into that cave with me. Walking into it with me will mean wrestling with me and not always understanding, but it will ultimately lead you to understand my own heart for this suffering. You will see how my heart grieves even more than yours does.*

If you choose the path of walking into that cave with me, together we will bring the light that is so desperately needed in that place. You are an ambassador of my love. My goodness is seen in those dark places if you choose to bring my goodness there.

Brad chose to go into that cave with God. He started iEmpathize (iempathize.org), an organization that is using innovative means such as films and art shows and grassroots movements to make this issue visible. It also provides safe homes for many rescued girls.

I think you can relate to this story if you have been through a divorce. Divorce is like your own personal cave. You can choose to walk into that cave *without* God, or you can choose to walk there *with* him. You can choose bitterness, or you can choose for your strength to clothe you and your lantern of love to go out before you, shedding God's light into that dark place.

If you have chosen to continue walking with God into that cave, I honor you. You have trusted in his goodness despite so much pain. If you are still a part of a church body, I commend you. Being in a community where you wonder if everyone looks at you as marked must be so difficult. You have chosen family over the fear of shame. You have chosen faith over bitterness. You are so strong.

If you are not divorced but are a part of a church body with divorced people, I believe you should go beyond just acknowledging and comforting them. I believe that divorced people should be listened to and even seen as wise. We need to recognize that these are people who have walked into their own personal cave and come out still believing in God's goodness. They have been through a difficult journey that has sharpened and molded them. They have the wisdom that only comes with experience. They understand how to love better a second time. We as a church need to humble ourselves and learn from their experience.

We need to see the scars. We should not ignore those scars and pretend they are not there. We should see them as part of journey in which that person came out of their cave still believing. Like Roger's scar, their wounds tell the story of their journey. And it is a story worth listening to.

12

Throw Away Your List (Or Just Rewrite It)

Ashley was shipwrecked on the Isle of Singleness. She was stranded there for a long time and was very lonely. She prayed, "God, please send a perfect man to get me off this island."

Soon, a man in a speedboat came along. He was very kind and dedicated. But he was listening to Celine Dion on the radio.

He said, "Ashley, I have come a very long way to take you off this island."

She told him, "Thanks for the offer, but God is going to send me the perfect man. And the perfect man cannot be listening to bad diva music."

Soon, another man came in a rowboat. He was great with children and had a wonderful sense of humor. But he was balding a little bit. He said, "My darling Ashley, I have rowed many hundreds of miles to rescue you off this island."

She replied, "I appreciate what you have done, but God is going to send me the perfect man to get me off this island. He has to have hair in all the right places. Namely a lot on his head and none on his back. Now why don't you just take your little bald head and row right back to the mainland."

Finally, a man came swimming to the shore. He had a huge heart and incredible faith. Breathless, he threw his arms around her and said, "Ashley, you are the woman of my dreams. I swam five hundred miles, and then I swam five hundred more just to be the man to swim a thousand miles and fall down at your door. I also strapped a romantic picnic dinner, your hairdryer, and your favorite chick flicks on my back."

Ashley replied, "What, no flowers?"

Ashley stayed on the island many years. Finally she shook her fist at the sky: "God, why haven't you sent me the perfect man to get me off this island?"

He said, "I sent you a potential husband in a speedboat, a potential husband in a rowboat, and a potential husband who swam a thousand miles to fall down at your door."

"But God," Ashley replied, "none of those men fit everything on my list!"

God said, "If you ever want to get off of this island, you're going to have to write a new list."*

I have a journal for my husband that I started when I was twenty-one. I poured my heart out to this journal. What was in my heart at the time was a considerable amount of romantic nonsense.

I haven't told many people this, but toward the beginning of this journal, I wrote a song for my future husband. It's called "Made as One." I wrote the first verse and the chorus, but I never wrote the second verse. On purpose. You know why? My plan was to write the second verse on the day my future husband asked me to marry him. I mean, how romantic is that? How much would my husband

---

* This is a little story I wrote based on a joke I've heard in church a few times. In the joke, a man is hanging on a branch, about to fall off a cliff into the ocean. He prays to God for help. He is subsequently sent different rescue missions, including two different boats and a helicopter. Each time he refuses the help, saying "God is going to save me." When he finally dies, he asks God why he wasn't given any help, and God says "I sent you two boats and a helicopter! What more did you want?!"

swoon when I sang it at our wedding? To hear this beautiful song that had been written for him over time, ending with the crescendo of our perfect union?

I secretly had a good idea of what the lines of that second verse would be, even though I was waiting to write them.

They would go something like this:

> It's been two years since I wrote those words
> You asked me to marry you tonight.
> I never knew my heart could feel like this
> I never knew our love could take such flight.

Or some such cheese.

But now that song will have to be different from what I expected. And it would be less catchy:

> It's been twelve years since I wrote those words
> Kind of funny we're middle aged
> If we had waited much longer, dear,
> You'd have to buy me some Bengay.

A lot of popular music genres have come and gone since I started the song, so now it sounds dated. In fact, now that I think about it, it sounds almost exactly like a bad Journey song.

I am not singing that thing at my wedding. No way.

And, of course, there is more than just the song in my journal. Tucked carefully away between the pages of that journal is…the list.

All you females out there, and probably a lot of the males, you know exactly what I'm talking about. You know what the list is because you have your own list. And I bet it's not too different from mine.

The list is a series of characteristics that I want in my future spouse. Here is a composite of a few items on my list and on the lists of some friends I interviewed:

1. He must be taller than me.

2. He must be strong.

3. He must have black hair and blue eyes.

4. He must have nice nails.

5. He must look good in a suit.

6. He must not watch a lot of football.

7. He has to love dogs.

8. He has to have a college education.

9. He has to be an avid reader.

10. He has to make a lot of money.

11. He must be willing to massage my feet.

12. He can never use the term "lol" in his texts.

13. He must not have hair on his chest.

14. He must not have any hair in his ears or nose or on his back. Ever.

15. He must have hair on his head.

16. He must be a pro-skiing, TV-avoiding, muscle-flexing, chore-doing, model-looking, eternal giver of romance and love and passion.

17. He can't snore.

18. Lastly, and under no circumstances, will I ever ever be intimate with someone who wears novelty socks.

Sound familiar?

Years ago a good friend of mine and I had some sparks flying around us for a while. One day, however, while eating lunch together, he started chewing with his mouth open a little bit. A man who chews with his mouth open was definitely not on my list. To make matters worse, he also had a pretty serious pimple on his face that day. Also not on my list.

So I ended up going for another guy who was much more suave than the first one. The second guy broke my heart after we dated for nine months. The pimple guy who chewed with his mouth open moved away and is now married with a few kids. He is an incredible dad, an incredible husband, and loves the Lord very much.

Sometimes, we don't see God's provision even when it is right in front of us because it looks different from what we expected.

I have quite a few things I would tell the younger version of myself, and this would be one of them: Marrying someone who has perfect table manners is not really going to matter in forty years. What is going to matter is that my partner is kind and has integrity and that we love being with each other.

I know now that habits can change. I can tell my partner that I'd feel loved if he tried not to show me the gumbo in his mouth. Table manners may be able to be tamed in just a few conversations. But turning a mean guy into a nice guy? A lifetime. Which one do I want on my list?

When we are young, we think there will always be potential suitors and that we need to wait for the perfect one. But at my age, we realize that dating should not be about finding someone perfect. It should be about finding a good match.

I had a forty-something male friend write me the other day about this very topic. He said, "Women at church seem to have a list that personifies their perfect man. These ladies won't take a risk on a guy who is not good-looking, who is balding, who can't play guitar, can't dance, or who has a gap in his teeth. All because of their list."

He went on to talk about how he has gone on a few dates with women who weren't believers. These women were much more open to actually seeing his heart, mostly because they didn't have their God-has-the-perfect-man-for-me glasses on. He didn't commit to these women, however, because he knew he couldn't compromise his faith. But, he reflected in his letter to me, he wished that he could find a woman with a strong faith who was also willing to see past his bald spot and into his heart. He concluded the letter saying, "Women want to be pursued, but not by a man who isn't handsome enough for them."

I don't want people to say, "Hey, that *Getting Naked Later* girl said I shouldn't be too picky or else I'll be thirty-something and alone. So I'd better marry my loser boyfriend as soon as possible." Therefore, I'm going to make myself very clear. When I say that you shouldn't be too picky, I am not saying you should compromise your deepest values and beliefs. I myself could have married quite a few men who would not have been good for me. Those break-ups were not about me being too picky; they were about me being smart. Even worse than marrying a man who is not a good fit is marrying someone who is toxic. Settling for a spouse who is unkind or severely addicted can be the most devastating decision of your life.

Let's learn not to be picky when it comes to the shallow things and to be very picky when it comes to the important things. That is the balance.

This point is well illustrated in this real-life letter sent to an advice columnist:

> Dear Amy,
>
> I've been dating a man on and off for at least fifteen years. He let me know on the first date that he's a "Confirmed Bachelor." I'm single too. Sometimes I don't hear from him for more than a year. And then he'll call to go out. Do you think I should always go out with him when he calls? I don't want to seem desperate. Also, do you think I should call him when I don't hear from him? I don't want him to think I'm a chaser. I like him very much and I find him very interesting to talk to. He's also very smart and I like a smart man…So far, we've had a very platonic relationship.[1]

You don't want to seem desperate? Sister, you've been waiting for this man for years. I've got news for you: You are desperate. He's interesting to talk to? Okay, you can check that off your list. He's smart? Fine, you can check that off too. But those two attributes are not enough on which build a relationship. You need to add a few things to your list, like *emotionally available* and *calls weekly instead of annually* and *doesn't tell me on the first date that he will never be committed to me.*

Why do we do this? Why do we skip over people who could be good for us just because we don't have "that gut feeling" from the first few dates? Why are we drawn to people we know are not good for us and stay with them? I think that in the first wakes of love, we convince ourselves that the latter group fits our list more than the first group. We convince ourselves that there is no one else for us.

When we're in love, it is hard to be practical. But we must force ourselves to be practical when making a decision that is this important.

A wise person will look for the fruit of something when it is still a seed. If you see deep-seated character issues—such as unkindness—that could be really difficult down the road, get out. I am serious. Out.

If fifteen of your dear friends tell you that they feel like your current relationship will really turn out to be a bad thing—that this guy you are dating is actually a jerk—they're probably seeing something you don't in your tunnel-of-love vision. Get out. I am serious. Out.

Where is the balance? What is the happy medium between having totally unrealistic expectations for anyone you date and marrying someone who will most likely be really hard to live with, who might even be a nightmare to live with?

In my opinion, one of the best solutions is to rewrite your list. Pare it down to four or five nonnegotiables.

Here are the nonnegotiables that I have chosen for my own spouse, if I do decide to get married.

1. He must have a deep love for God and for people.

2. He must be kind.

3. We need to enjoy being with each other. Evidence of this would be laughing together, having good conversations, and dealing with conflict well.

4. He needs to see the world as a place to explore and as a place to bring hope. I want his vision to be to bring love to the community around us, whether that be in small ways or big ways. I honestly couldn't care less if we make a lot of money. That is not a priority for me. My priority is that we make the world a better place together.

I can't think of much else that matters other than the qualities on my new short list. Balding? He can shave his head—that can be sexy. Chewing with his mouth open? We can talk about that. Celine Dion? He can listen to her on his earphones all his heart desires. Snoring? I can wear earplugs. If he has the qualities that are on my new list, I will go on some dates with him. I will give him a chance.

I know that writing a new list is not a foolproof plan for finding a quality spouse. I realize that many of you out there married someone you thought was a really good choice but turned out not to be. I understand that we can't see the future. But we can try our best to look for the fruit of something while it is still a seed. Give your seed time to grow. That way you can consciously make a commitment using both your heart and your head.

A little eight-year-old girl was asked what she thought love was. She cocked her head and thought for a little bit. Then she replied, "When my grandmother got arthritis, she couldn't bend over to paint her toenails anymore. So my grandfather does it for her all the time, even when his hands got arthritis. That's what love is."[2]

Look for someone who will love you like this little girl's grandpa loved his wife. Look for a seed that will end in this kind of fruit. Don't just look for a spouse who you are lightning-flash attracted to. Don't just look for someone who says all the perfect things at the perfect time and gives you dozens of roses. Don't just look for someone who fits everything on your ridiculously long, shallow list. Look for someone who will paint your toenails when you're old even though he has arthritis.

Because that's what love is.

Kate's Corner of Wisdom

How to Date

1. Go out; give them a chance.
2. Set clear boundaries. Communicate well.
3. Get good information day by day.
4. When you have enough information to know if it's a good match or not, decide whether to get married or break up.

90s Dating Gone Bad

In the late 90s and early 2000s, a series of books in the Christian market discussed different reasons dating might be a bad, even ungodly, idea. They suggested that Christians should try something called "courting" instead of dating, which involved going on group dates instead of individual dates.

The cover of the most popular book, *I Kissed Dating Goodbye,* had a picture of a man with a mysterious hat over his eyes and a very, very nice jawline. I really wanted to date him. On the back of the book was a snapshot of the very handsome young author (only 22 at the time) looking wistfully into the camera with his innocent brown eyes. Definitely wanted to date him too. If Christian book publishers really wanted me to stop dating, they should have put less attractive guys on the cover.

These books turned into a Christian phenomenon that turned into a bunch of rules that turned into a tsunami from whose wake the Christian dating pool is still recovering. Even though the rules that were established in the era of these books were much more popular 20 years ago, their weirdness still affects us. We have become the Frankenstein children of bad 90s dating. Being aware of the rules that fell into place during this era will help us understand why some of us have green skin and bolts coming out of our necks when we date.

Let's look at some of the rules of this "no dating tolerance" era and learn from them so we can date better now.

Rule #1: God needs to tell us, often through signs, whom we are going to marry.

About ten years ago, my boyfriend, Ken, and I were contemplating marriage. I was as scared as a pregnant porcupine.

Back then, I would pray for signs all the time: "God, if you really want me to marry him, please have someone stand on their head in the middle of this convenience store." Stuff like that.

I fasted several times for the relationship, begging for signs from God. I did one especially long fast during which I started out with water only. Soon, I was throwing cherry pie into the blender. I was on the verge of trying a steak smoothie when I finally got my answer in the middle of the night. I had a dream that I opened my Bible to 4 Chronicles.

That was the whole dream.

I woke up the next day, and, being the astute Christian scholar that I am, I realized that there is, in fact, no 4 Chronicles. So I looked up 1 Chronicles 4 instead.

These were the shocking words I read that day: "Reaiah the son of Shobal begat Jahath; and Jahath begat Ahumai, and Lahad. These are the families of the Zorathites" (1 Chronicles 4:2 KJV).

Bingo. That was it. I was supposed to marry him.

Okay, that's not really what happened. I was more like, "What the heck is this? Come on, God. I wanted a sign, and I got a bunch of begets!"

Almost as a joke, I said, "God, if I'm supposed to marry Ken, put a version of his name in here." I turned the page, and there it was clear as day. "These were the men of Rechah. And the sons of Kenaz..." (1 Chronicles 4:12-13 KJV). Kenaz certainly sounded like the Hebrew version of Ken to me. I had my answer.

What happened next? I'll give you one hint: I'm still single, and it's ten years later.

Another serious boyfriend and I—let's call him Jordan—were praying about whether we should get married. During the course of our relationship, he had struggled with whether he loved me or not. We had separated into different cities for a season—you know, the whole "we're taking a break to pray" deal that actually means "we're freaking out." We had met together to reevaluate, and he said he wanted to move to my town and pursue our relationship one more time. I was worried that he would still struggle with whether or not he loved me, and so I was hesitant.

Jordan and I decided to pray about it for a few weeks. In the meantime, I looked for signs like a nearsighted truck driver.

I got the sign I was looking for when I went to visit my mom and we played a game of Boggle together. If you haven't seen Boggle before, it has a covered tray of 16 dice with letters on them. You shake the dice, and they fall into place on the grid of the tray. Players compete to find short words.

My mom and I played one round in which, clear as day, she found the words "Jordan is in love" on the little squares. I mean, out of thousands of combinations of letters, those were the ones that happened to be rolled. I have the picture to prove it. What are the odds of that?

I had my sign, and my mom had 20 more Boggle points. Despite the sign, Jordan and I broke up three weeks later.

A year after we broke up, I showed some friends a picture of the Boggle game. They looked at the picture carefully.

"Oh yeah! There's 'Jordan,' see it? And there's 'is' and 'in' and 'love.' That is crazy, Kate!"

They passed the Boggle picture on to my friend Aaron, who noticed something important: "Kate, there is another word in here that you missed. The word 'not.'"

I looked at the picture, and, sure enough, there it was—a very important word I had missed for an entire year: n-o-t.

Depending on how astute I was at the game of Boggle, I could have read the sentence "Jordan is in love" or "Jordan is not in love." Wow. Can you spell D-A-N-G-E-R-O-U-S?

We often look for signs that tell us what we want to see. When it comes to something as important as marriage, this is a risky way to make decisions. The truth is, a sign might be good information, but it's not even close to all the information you need to assess whether or not a person is a wise choice for a future mate.

The moral of the story? Don't let a Boggle game tell your future. It can be dangerous to rely completely on signs without tempering those signs with practical wisdom. It can also be immature.

First Corinthians 13:11 says, "When I was a child, I talked like a child, I thought like a child, I reasoned like a child. When I became a man, I put the ways of childhood behind me." You may tell a little child "don't touch that" when they are about to stick their finger in a light socket, but when that child becomes an adult, you know that person is wise enough not to touch the light socket. In the same way, when we become spiritually mature enough to self-govern, it's time to move on to a new model for dating—one that goes beyond signs and becomes suitable for thinking adults. One in which we make decisions with God instead of having him make decisions for us.

Rule # 2: Dating isn't biblical.

It's true that dating isn't biblical. It's not in the Bible. So maybe we should try a marriage philosophy that is in the Bible: polygamy. Abraham had one wife and one concubine. David had lots more. Solomon was the wisest man on earth, and he pretty much had an entire motel full of them. That's in the Bible, so it must be biblical. Taking up this biblical marriage practice would solve a lot of problems. We all know there are probably about ten Christian women for every Christian man. If we just started practicing this tradition, voilà! Problem solved!

Of course, I'm exaggerating. We understand that polygamy is not a good idea. We understand that the practice was a part of Hebrew and surrounding cultures (mostly in the upper class), but that it was never necessarily God's best. Just because something is in the Bible doesn't mean that it's right. And conversely, just because something is not in the Bible doesn't mean it's wrong.

American culture is different from the culture of the Bible. When my dad wants to buy some land, he doesn't offer my hand in marriage along with 20 camels and a flock of sheep. Marriage is no longer a business proposition the way it used to be. It's a search for a life companion.

Women are now able to make enough money to support themselves, and, thus, they are not required to have a husband in order to survive. (Indeed, throughout history there were few alternatives for livelihood for women besides marriage and prostitution.) Women's rights have been one of the major factors that have brought us from a culture of arranged marriages to a culture in which people date to find a mate. Therefore, dating is not necessarily a bad institution; rather, it's an institution that has progressed as marriage has changed. An institution that now allows for a woman's choice rather than a woman's obedience.

Those who favor courtship over dating may argue that the way the Western world dates now ends in a 50 percent divorce rate. I would absolutely agree with them. Dating in the modern world can often be fixated on sexual attraction rather than truly searching to find a well-suited life partner. Many people sleep around as if sex were as much of a commitment as buying a cup of coffee in the morning. When that attraction fades, the commitment can fade along with it. Marriage in popular culture seems to have lost some of its sacredness. It's often joked about. I know that this is not the best way. Jesus weeps when relationships are this broken, and so do I.

At the same time, I don't want to go back to a time in which I am seen as a commodity—a time in which I have no say in a decision as important as marriage. Yes, I agree that dating is an institution that has been abused, but I don't believe that because people around me are abusing it or the media is abusing it that I have to abuse it.

Instead of seeing dating as unhealthy because it is not in the Bible or because people around us have abused it, perhaps we can use it as an effective tool in choosing a good partner. Perhaps we can have good boundaries in dating. Perhaps we can learn a lot about ourselves and about which match would make sense for us. Perhaps we can make wise, educated decisions because we have spent good time with different people and, ultimately, with the person we commit ourselves to. Dating can be useful in our journeys of marrying well…if we use it the right way.

Rule #3: You should never be alone with the person you are dating because you don't want to end up having premarital sex.

You may have noticed that for a book that has the word "naked" in the title, I have written very little on these pages about sex. At first I felt I should have at least one chapter dedicated to that subject, but then I realized I am actually quite private when it comes to those things.

To be perfectly honest, I don't know a lot about sex. I don't know enough to write a whole chapter on the subject, let alone a whole book. (Which, I guess, is what you might have been expecting when you picked up this book. Sorry if I disappointed you.)

But I do think I can muster up a few paragraphs. Here goes…

I have lived my life with the philosophy that sex is sacred. So sacred, in fact, that I have chosen to be that intimate only with someone inside the boundaries of a lifelong covenant. I have made that choice not simply because it's what my Christian culture expects me to do; I have chosen it because I know having sex with a man (or several men over the course of time) who are not in covenant with me would be very, very hard on my heart. I also know that having sex could put me in difficult situations I may not be prepared for. I want to be wise when it comes to what I do with my body. It's the only body I have, after all.

I have also chosen abstinence because covenant is serious to God, and there is nothing else on earth that seals a covenant in the same way sex does. This is why it is especially devastating that our modern society treats sex so casually. Many people have taken something mysterious and sacred and have turned it into something common. That is infinitely sad to me, and it is infinitely sad to the God who created that sacred union. I have chosen to see sex as sacred because my God sees it as sacred. If that means waiting, I will wait.

Yes, there are days when abstinence is a difficult choice. There are days when society makes me feel as if I'm not a whole person because I haven't had sex. There are days in springtime when I wonder if every adult animal in the world is having sex except me. There are days when a man touches my arm for just a second, and I realize how good it feels to have someone's skin on mine. And then I remember how seldom touch is a part of my life, and I realize how much I ache to have someone hold me.

Despite these things, for the most part, I have found abstinence to be a good choice for me. I think waiting for marriage is a good way to live, and I can back that up with my own choices.

After saying all that, I have to add that the 90s dating-gone-bad rules were very odd when it came to sex. The rules said that we should always group date or date in public. How are we ever supposed to get to know someone that way? Will we go to such lengths to avoid having sex that we march our innocent little butts down the aisle toward a person we barely know? Sex before marriage can be destructive, but so can marrying a person whose middle name you don't know until you are on your honeymoon.

Even though I think it's essential to get to know a potential mate and be alone with them, it's important to have some boundaries set into place. I don't think I could handle the practice that some Amish communities have of "bundling" or "bed courting," which involves a courting couple sleeping in the same bed as long as both people are clothed and the woman has the sheets to herself.[1] I'm not sure if this would be a good rule for me. My inner dragon might come out in that situation. And my inner dragon is not Amish.

As always, there needs to be balance. Balance between understanding the sacredness of sex and understanding the sacredness of knowing someone very well when you tie yourself to them for life.

Here are two things that I think will help us in the quest for good physical boundaries when we date.

The first is to "know thyself."

These are Plato's words, and they are full of wisdom. Try to understand what is going on inside you when it comes to sex. Figure out what you can handle.

In my case, I know I can make a boundary with someone I am dating and stick with it. I can kiss and have a lot of fun and intimacy, and I can back off and communicate when I think we might cross the boundaries we have set. Letting myself have beautiful moments of intimacy with men I have dated seriously but still keeping my boundaries has actually been healing for me. I have gone through certain things in my past that made me apprehensive of any kind of intimacy, but over the years I have dated trustworthy, kind men who respected the boundaries we set together, and God has brought a lot of healing through that, even though I didn't marry any of those men. I now really enjoy intimacy instead of being scared of it.

On the other hand, there may be some who cannot handle much physical intimacy. Some folks want to make a sprint around the bases if their partner wears the right cologne. Be honest with yourself. Communicate well with the person you are dating. Make boundaries together that you know you can follow.

The second thing that will help us in our quest for good physical boundaries is to foster a culture that does not succumb to the lie that we are slaves to sin.

Now, I don't want to downplay a subject that has been a lifelong struggle for some people. I don't really understand what it's like to be someone who has been tortured by sex addictions or pornography. (Let me say that I applaud you for being brave and fighting for freedom from this.) I know that sex before marriage is tempting. I know that we need good boundaries. But I believe that one of the best ways to deal with this issue is to stop seeing ourselves as weak. We have to stop telling ourselves that if we are left to our own devices we will have no choice but to lose ourselves to passion. We have to stop acting as though sexual desire is a force that takes over us and that we have no choice but to kneel as its slave.

If we see ourselves as people who have no control over ourselves, then we will be people who have no control over ourselves. We should start seeing ourselves for what we are: people whom the Lord has made strong. People who have self-control and who do not need chastity belts in order to be in the same room with someone of the opposite sex. The more we see ourselves as weak, the weaker we will be. We must remember the truth: Temptation does not have control over us. We have control over temptation.

I know it is unwise to sleep in the same bed or to go off for the weekend to some romantic place and think we won't be tempted. We don't want to set ourselves up to cross our boundaries, and there is something special about saving those activities for covenant. However, let's see ourselves as people who can have adult dating relationships that allow us to get to know each other very, very well before we get married without having to tear each other's clothes off before the wedding night.

Self-governing is always the kind of government that works the best, and this is especially true when it comes to sex.

Rule #4: You should know whether you will get married or not within the first few dates.

This is the rule that has seeped into our dating landscape more than any other. Men have an especially large amount of pressure on them in this regard when it comes to dating. If a man finally gets up the nerve to ask out someone they like, it's likely that, as a result of this silly rule, the bridesmaids' dresses and china patterns are picked out after the first cup of coffee. Christian men often find themselves in a quandary, thinking, "I want to get to know this girl, but if I ask her out, I need to be pretty sure I'm serious about her. But how do I know if I am serious about her if I don't spend quality time with her?" It is a catch-22. I would be scared too. See what a bunch of rules does to us?

I once heard a lecture by Biola University professor John Coe in which he compared men and women in this situation to Peter Pan and Cinderella. Read the letters I imagine might have passed between the two and you will see why:

∽ Letter from Cinderella to Peter Pan ∂⌒

Dear Peter,

We have now been on three dates. I loved our time flying to Never-Never Land. (I especially liked it the second time, when Wendy didn't tag along.) Flying with you was so romantic. My heart has been fluttery for days. I must admit I got my hopes up.

I have given you all the right hints and flirty moves. But today when I texted you, it took you two hours to text me back!

So, Peter, you need to get your act together. Either you want me or you don't. I am beautiful and a great catch, and *underneath it all I am a princess*!!!

The bottom line, Peter, is that you need to GROW UP!

Sincerely,
Your Lady in Waiting
Cinderella

꩜ *Letter from Peter Pan to Cinderella* ꩜

Dear Cinderella,

Let me give a you a peek into my heart. In my churchgoing world, people often expected really intense commitment really fast. This scared me. So I habitually stayed in the "friend zone" with girls…spending lots of time with them and getting them to like me so I could feel good. I was afraid of getting out of the friend zone because, according to my culture, that meant I should be ready to get married.

I would much rather stay a boy than face this much pressure. I was stunted in my dating life. I wasn't really growing up.

I finally decided that my rules were not working well for me, so I took a plunge into the dating pool. I have gone out on some dates to get to know people and even to challenge myself to get out of the friend zone.

One lady had seven little people living with her. I found that to be a little strange, so I decided to move on. Another one was sleeping the whole time. I could tell she wanted me to kiss her to wake her up, but I wasn't ready to kiss someone I hadn't talked to yet.

You have been my favorite so far. You are beautiful and strong, you love animals, and you have a great singing voice. You're a lot taller than me, but I can work with that.

Cinderella, here is the problem. I feel so much pressure from you and all of these other girls. The *I Kissed Dating Goodbye* culture taught me that I should only date someone if I know I am going to marry them. This put enormous amounts of stress even on a first date. It has scared all of us men out of wanting to date anyone at all.

When you say to me "either you want me or you don't," that makes me feel backed against a wall. I *do* like you, very much, but I need good time with you to really know whether we are a good match or not.

I am not into dating casually, but I am into dating slow. Can you see the difference?

Sincerely,
Peter
P.S. I think you left a shoe at my place.

To all of you Cinderellas out there, maybe you need to give Peter time without pressure for him to get to know you. Help him feel safe. Don't try to make him fill this insatiable desire in you to feel valued. Calm down all of that franticness and trust God. Only he can give you the value you are looking for, and truly living in that place will make Peter feel so much more freedom to get to know you and love you well if that is the plan God has for you.

To all of you Peter Pans, try not to do what you did to Wendy and Tinker Bell, just leading them on. Take time to learn if you really like this girl or not. Be clear with her how you are feeling. After time, if you are not into her, let her go. If you are into her, take steps to further commit to her.

The pressure from the rule of "you should know within the first few dates" is exacerbated by the "I just knew" phenomenon. We have all heard stories like, "I saw him across the fellowship hall as he was eating his doughnut. We started discussing predestination, and I knew then and there that I was predestined for him. We were married three months later." Sure, this not-so-imaginary couple knew what they wanted right away and got it. But I wonder if those are also the kind of decisive people who see an outfit they like in the department store window, try it on, and immediately buy it. That decisiveness could be the way they make all their decisions. I, on the other hand, look at an outfit in several different mirrors for half an hour before I decide if I want it, and after I buy it I still save my receipt for six months just in case I change my mind. I seem to date the same way.

The point is, we all have different decision-making methods, and we will probably use those when we date. For every "I just knew" story, there is an "I didn't think I liked him at all until I got to know him" story. If we give up right away because we want someone else's story, we might miss out on the beautiful relationship that is uniquely meant for us.

Clearly, the combined formula of the "you shouldn't date unless you know" rule and the "you should know right away" rule puts enormous pressure on the first stages of dating, a time I think should start out as casual and fun.

In my opinion, it's far too dangerous to rush things when you are making a decision this important. When we date, we should take the time to know someone in the day-to-day, getting good information until there is enough to make a wise choice. Like Peter said, there is a big difference between dating casually and dating slow.

I have heard over and over again in my interviews with married people that putting pressure on oneself to "know" after the first few dates can be dangerous because it could mean rushing to get married too soon. I have tried to put that advice into practice by using a little tool I call the "holiday effect." I ask myself if there is enough enjoyment and beauty and mutual sharpening in this relationship that I would want to keep pursuing it to the next holiday. If the answer is yes, I invest wholeheartedly in the relationship day-by-day until the next holiday, and then I check what is going on with us as a couple and what is going on inside of me. I ask myself if we are a good match, if I am having fun, if the person I'm dating has integrity, and if I am feeling hesitant because we are not a good match or because I'm scared of commitment. After I ask those questions, I keep doing the next best thing. I try not to think about marriage until I'm far along in this process. Someday I will get enough information to know whether a future with this person is a good idea or not. Thinking this way helps keep myself in check if I find myself thinking about marriage too soon.

Marriage is serious business. A decision this important deserves respect and time. Getting good information is important. I believe that the clearest way God can speak to us, rather than through signs similar to those we talked about earlier, is through us answering practical questions over time. How does my boyfriend treat his mother? How does my girlfriend handle stress? Am I terrified of committing? Why is that? Is my boyfriend kind to people even in difficult circumstances? Does my girlfriend make God a part of her everyday life? Do we love each other even when our projections of each other have been lowered? Are my negative experiences with my family of origin affecting our relationship? Can we work to heal together by getting good counsel? Do we have fun together? Do we communicate well?

These are questions that take time to answer. Do not rush in answering them. Let's not let all of these rules dictate something as important as whom we are going to marry. Let's not let fear be the driving force behind dating. Instead, let's allow God's love and wisdom to lead us every step of the way.

Hold the Ones You Love

The most beautiful thing we can experience is
the mysterious. It is the source of all true art and
science. He to whom this emotion is a stranger, who
can no longer pause to wonder and stand rapt in
awe, is as good as dead; his eyes are closed.

Albert Einstein

A few months ago I went to Washington to play a few concerts and visit my friend Carson. It was impossible for me to know as I boarded the plane that when I got back to Colorado a month later (almost three weeks later than I had planned), I would see the whole world differently.

Carson has a very rare disease called Budd-Chiari syndrome, which is a fancy way of saying that his bone marrow produces too many blood platelets, making his blood too thick. It is a one-in-a-million disease, and he has an even rarer form of it, known as a JAK2 mutation, that was discovered only a few years ago.

The Bible says that "the life of every creature is in its blood" (Leviticus 17:14) and I have never seen this more clearly illustrated than in Carson's sickness. If his blood stays thick, it will clot and he could die, so he has to take blood thinners. But if his blood gets too thin he will throw up lots and lots of blood.

Carson was diagnosed with Budd-Chiari eleven years ago, at

which time the doctors said he had ten years to live. Despite all his health problems, he lives every day well. I have never met anyone who has suffered so much with their health, yet I have never heard him complain. He makes a conscious effort to live every day in the moment, to remember the preciousness of life and the people around him. He knows it's possible that he won't have many moments left. Until his health recently worsened, in fact, he rafted and hiked and rock-climbed. His favorite thing is "flying," his word for paragliding, which he has done all over the world.

Before he was diagnosed, Carson worked at a boy's home in Denver called Lost and Found. Soon he felt working at the facility was not enough; he didn't want only to be a mentor to these troubled kids. He wanted to be a father to them. He knew that someday he wanted to adopt.

After he was diagnosed, he still longed to take care of kids who needed a dad. He didn't want to hold off doing foster care until he got married because he knew his days might be limited. He came up with a unique solution: He started taking in older foster kids alongside his platonic friend, Trish, knowing that having two adults would be the safest way to care for the kids with his health problems. Carson and Trish have never been romantically involved, but they work and live together to take care of these kids.

One day, the state asked them to take in a three-year-old named Collin for a little while. Originally, Carson and Trish had agreed not to take younger children, but they had a peace about it this time and accepted. Even at such a young age, Collin had the biggest personality you could imagine, bringing laughter and joy to everyone around him. His older brother, Avie, who is so kind and wise that you have to remember that he is ten and not twenty-two, came to live with them a few months later.

Inevitably, Carson and Trish ended up loving these two brothers. Collin and Avie's birth mother really wanted the pair to take her sons. Carson and Trish were in a quandary: Should they let these kids be put back in the foster care system or should they take the boys as their own even though Carson could die?

The answer was clear. They loved the boys too much to put them back in the foster care system. So the state let them adopt the boys, fully aware that Carson and Trish were platonic friends. Theirs is a family like no other I've met, and their circumstances seem odd to people who don't know them well. But when you spend time with them, you realize that despite the nontraditional nature of their family, those boys are deeply loved.

I had a very special week visiting Carson and Trish in Washington a few years ago. But the sweetness ended abruptly when, one morning at 4:00, Trish came into my room and turned on the light. She asked me if I could take care of the boys as Carson had just thrown up a lot of blood and needed to go to the hospital.

The next 24 hours were a nightmare. At the first local hospital, Carson lost so much blood that they almost ran out of bags of his type to transfuse. If the helicopter had come in any later to take him to Seattle, they would have run out and he could have died.

Trish and I stayed up all night looking at pictures of Carson and the boys, and the next day we drove to Seattle to see him in the hospital. When we got there, we walked into a room with three doctors and some other family members. They sat us down and very somberly told us that Carson would never see or talk to us again, but that he might be able to hear us. He was going to die in the next 24 hours.

Sobbing, I called many friends to pray. Two people said, "Kate, you have been in this place before. Your nephew almost died when he was born, and you were on the road to dying or being severely disabled with Lyme disease. It is not a mistake that you were visiting this week. You are there for a reason."

My spiritual father, Chuck, told me, "You need to help Carson's family take their eyes off the problem and onto the goodness of God."

I marched into Carson's room, where he was unconscious and on a respirator that looked like a hockey mask. I don't know where I got the courage, but I went right up to him, grabbed his hand, and started singing songs over him. There were family members in the room that I had never met before who were probably wondering who I was, but I didn't care. I was going to worship God in the midst of this tragedy. I was going to speak life over him.

Carson's mom, Cheryl, had her head in Carson's lap and was crying. When I started singing, she looked up and started singing with me, even though she didn't know the words to the song.

The doctors told Carson's family that they should tell him that it was okay for him to die, that Trish and the boys would be taken care of. I didn't want to go against his family or the wishes of the doctors, but I had a hard time doing what they had asked. So I woke up in the middle of the night and sang songs about life over him for about two hours, and I told him he wasn't going to die.

I told Carson he was going to see Avie and Collin get married and he was going to meet his grandkids. Even writing such a strong encouragement now is difficult because I know Carson still has many complications. I didn't (and don't) want to give false hope, but when I said those words to him I could clearly see him in a chair with all his grandkids around him, telling stories. There was hope in that hospital room that night—a hope so tangible I could almost touch it. When you are at someone's deathbed, you stop taking that person for granted. The wonder and mystery of Carson lay in that bed. The threat of losing him made me remember how precious he is, how precious my life is.

The next morning, Carson started to stabilize. He could motion to us, indicating that he was semi-conscious. The doctors were practically in shock. They had been sure that he would die, saying that they had never seen anyone with insides like his. He had lost incredible amounts of blood in the last 24 hours. How could he possibly be waking up?

Friday was the day he was supposed to die. By Monday, he was eating and sitting up. He even walked into the waiting room, still attached to his IV, to surprise all of us. He waved at the nurses and the doctors as he walked by, and they looked at him in disbelief. They had thought that his name wouldn't have been on the door by the end of the previous weekend, and here he was walking around.

Wednesday of that week was Avie's birthday. Carson cleaned up, got his hair cut, and put on some new clothes. We hung balloons all over the ICU waiting room, and we bought pizzas, cake, and gifts for Avie. We invited the doctors and nurses and loved ones of the people in the ICU to the party. A place of despair had become a place of hope and laughter.

The boys had been told that weekend that Carson, their father, was going to die. But now they knew there was still hope. When the boys arrived at the hospital, Avie and Collin waited at the end of the hallway for their dad to come to them. He walked toward them. I remember it in slow motion. When he got to them, he threw his arms around them and started sobbing.

At the end of the party, Carson went to every person in the room, even people he had never met, kissed them on the cheek, and told them he loved them.

I stayed with Carson and his family for two and half weeks in the hospital. We would spend at least ten hours a day there. Every day I called as many people I could think of to pray, and I was on the phone for hours at a time. People all over the world prayed for Carson. Friends who had never met him would cry with me on the phone. Because his life was dear to me, his life was dear to them.

I wrote two songs for Carson while I was with him in the hospital. The first was about him flying, about how beautiful it was to see someone in the midst of the sorrow of disease choose to live with joy. My favorite lyric is this: "You have taken your sorrows and turned them into wings." That line captures who he is.

I also wrote a song for him and his family. These are some of the lyrics:

When all is said and done
Sometimes we forget how precious life is
Until it's nearly gone
So hold the ones you love
Hold the ones you love
I will not take for granted
How life surrounds me like air
From this day forward
I will hold the ones I love
Hold the ones I love
And oh, how precious life is
And oh, how precious life is.

You realize both the beauty and the difficulty of life when you are in a hospital. Everything bad gets magnified and everything good gets magnified. Life feels so precious. Life feels so hard. Everyone around you seems beautiful, but everything around you seems tragic. As Steven Galloway said in his book *The Cellist of Sarajevo*, "It's a rare gift to understand that your life is wondrous, and that it won't last forever."[1]

When I finally came home to Boulder while Carson waited for a liver transplant, I was in a state of wonder for a few days. I almost kissed the kind grocery clerk on the cheek, and I wanted to give the homeless woman begging on the street a huge hug. I wondered why anyone would fight with each other, why every day was not a day that we would celebrate the beauty in one another.

David James Duncan writes that "Wonder is unknowing experienced as pleasure. Wonder is a period at the end of a statement we've long taken for granted, suddenly looking up and seeing the sinuous curve of a tall black hat on its head, and realizing it was a question mark all along. Wonder is anything taken for granted—the old neighborhood, old job, old buddy, old spouse—suddenly filling with mystery. Wonder is anything closed suddenly opening…it is wonder, more than courage, that conquers fear of death."[2]

Carson got a liver transplant a few weeks after I left and was able to get out of the hospital on Christmas day. He still has complications, and we all keep praying for him. But he is alive. It seems that his wonder—even more than his courage—has conquered his fear of death. The doctors told us that they have seldom seen anyone survive something like what he went through. The world has been given a gift because Carson is still alive.

Carson's story teaches us an important lesson about our relationships, especially those of our close family members and the spouses and children we may one day have. The lesson is this: Normal life—non-deathbed life—is what we live most days. We often take people for granted. In a very literal way, we think that our loved ones are granted to us. That they are in our possession and that we will never lose them. Instead of remembering how precious someone is, we forget. Instead of focusing on the mystery of the essence of a person, we focus on the fact that the trash has not been taken out. Instead of remembering every right thing that someone has done, we remember every wrong thing. We forget and we forget and we forget.

Recently, while on my quest to gain wisdom from married couples, I sat down with my friends Matt and Amanda. I asked if they had any advice for me. Matt answered, "When I first married Amanda, it was my commitment to talk about her in a positive light. This didn't mean that I couldn't be honest and process my marriage with friends. It just meant that I committed to saying loving things about her when she was in the room with me and when she was somewhere else. After a while, though, I learned that talking about Amanda positively was not enough. I needed to commit to seeing her positively too. She is such a beautiful person, and if I don't choose every day to see that, I will take her for granted. Now I make a conscious effort to notice her uniqueness and beauty every day."

Like Matt, I want to posture my heart toward seeing the

beautiful. I want to make a commitment in my heart to remember. If I do ever get married and on the occasions when romance is lacking and there are children and bills and mundaneness, I want to look at my husband and see the mystery of who he is. I want to call to mind all the kindness and complexity and commitment and laughter and looks and caresses and beautiful history that are wrapped up into this person God has given me. I want to be aware that this person is not merely granted to me, but there are limited days in his life and I should appreciate the gift of the days I spend with him.

For today, even before I am married, I have dear friends who are also mysteries. They have laughed with me over meals and cried with me over breakups. Each person is so precious. I want to remember. Even though I am no longer in the wake of a near-death experience, there are still people on the street who are lonely, like that homeless women who needed a hug. Maybe this time, I should just hug her.

I also want to remember that there is a God who cannot be contained by eternity and who listens to me every day when I pray. There is one who sees me beautiful, who doesn't take me for granted. He created universes I can't begin to understand, but he also created a leaf with tiny lines on it that I can hold in my hand. That's how personal he is. I don't want to take him for granted, either. Looking at him for one moment would change my life. It would take a lifetime to fully take in one tiny part of him. That's how full of wonder he is.

Life is precious. The people in my life are precious. My God is precious. Help me remember, Lord. Help me remember.

When all is said and done, sometimes we forget how precious life is until it's nearly gone. So hold the ones you love. Hold the ones you love.

Pity Parties and Prodigals

I would like to devote this chapter to an important ritual single people practice: the pity party. I have been the event planner for quite a few of these festivities, so I can talk about them with some expertise.

Okay, I'll stop being modest and just say it: I am the Martha Stewart of pity parties. Here are some of my pity party planning tips:

1. Come depressed. Your goal should be to obsess about how crappy your life is and have your guests comfort you as you talk about how crappy your life is.

2. Be selective about who you invite. Don't include people who will say things like, "Get over yourself" or "It's time to move on." They will ruin everything.

3. Wear the proper outfit. This usually includes glasses, pajamas, and rabbit slippers.

4. Plan your menu. I like to have potato chips as my appetizer, Ben & Jerry's as the main course, and maybe another kind of Ben & Jerry's for dessert. An assortment of deep-fried foods works great for side dishes. If

you want to get especially fancy, add a garnish of
marshmallows and Tootsie Rolls.

5. Prepare your music. Mood music is very important! I
   have a mix tape labeled "Kate's Songs That Allow Her
   to Wallow in the Depths of Despair." This tape contains
   such classics as "All By Myself," made popular by our
   mentor, Bridget Jones, "Nothing Compares to You" by
   Sinead O Connor, "I Will Survive" by Gloria Gaynor,
   and "I'm Too Sexy" by Right Said Fred. (Wait, how did
   that get on here?)

6. Plan some really fun games! My favorites are "Pin the
   Tail on the Ex-Boyfriend" and "Hit the Piñata that
   Looks Remarkably Like Someone I Used to Kiss."

7. Make sure to light lots of candles. If the pity party goes
   well, you and your guests can use them to burn your
   love notes and pictures. For a more memorable finale,
   build a bonfire and have everyone bring their own pity
   party memorabilia to throw into it. That way you can
   wallow in heartache as a community. What a great way
   to bond!

8. If you want to provide party favors, I can hook you up
   with some nice pity party T-shirts. I have soft gray ones
   that you can wear to bed, hot pink ones with sparkles
   that come in sets of three for when you go out with the
   girls, and light blue ones that have "Pity Party" very
   subtly written on them that are especially nice to wear
   to church. I also have pity party mugs and pity party
   signature Kleenex.

Follow these tips, and you too can have a great (read: pathetic
and soul-draining) pity party!

In all seriousness, the reason I am such an expert is that I have thrown many pity parties lately. In fact, these pity parties grew to a climax when my long-time counselor recently challenged me to examine what I would do if I never got married and didn't have biological children. How would I rearrange my life if my only choice in having a child were to adopt? She also asked me if I thought that my life would still be valuable if I never had a traditional family. It was very difficult for me to say yes.

I was devastated after this counseling session. I felt really sorry for myself, but I also recognized how much my thoughts about remaining single and childless have consumed me lately. I haven't been sleeping very well. My mind has been mulling over my difficult childhood, wondering if it contributed to a man not falling in love with me. I have been bitter toward ex-boyfriends for rejecting me. I have been doubting God's goodness and even his existence because he has not given me this, one of my deepest desires.

In other words, I have been trying to blame anyone I can for my pain.

This difficult counseling session helped purge the deep sadness in me, and it also made me realize that I am spiritually "hung over" and exhausted from all the pity parties I have been throwing for myself.

In the midst of all these revelations about myself, I read a passage in the Bible that depicted someone who threw one of the best pity parties in the New Testament: the older brother in the story of the prodigal son.

In this well-known and wonderful story, we see a family with two sons: the young, rebellious son and the elder, religious son.

The younger son demands his share of the estate from his father and leaves home after his father complies with his request. In that day, it was an act of disdain for a son to demand his inheritance before his father died. Essentially, the younger son says to his father, "All I want from you is the gifts you can give. I don't want your love; I want your loot."

After the younger son leaves and lives a life of debauchery, he sees that his life away from home is nothing like he expected. He squanders his money and becomes poor and lonely. He is hired to feed pigs and craves the pods the pigs are eating. In his hunger, he realizes that even the servants in his father's house had never been as hungry as he was. He recognizes that he has a good father and that it was his own selfishness that got him into his place of need.

He decides to go back home, but because of the way he left, he has no hope that his father will welcome him back as a son. He truly believes that the only way his father would take him back is if he were to return home as a slave. He even creates a speech to give his father at his return:

"'Father, I have sinned against heaven and against you. I am no longer worthy to be called your son; make me like one of your hired men.' So he got up and went to his father" (Luke 15:18-20).

In one of the most beautiful illustrations of love in scripture and in any other literature, the father sees his son coming from afar and gives up all his dignity by running out to greet the young man as he walks the road home. The father throws his arms around his son and kisses him.

The younger son tries to deliver his speech, saying, "Father, I have sinned against heaven and against you. I am no longer worthy to be called your son."

But the father says to his servants, "'Quick! Bring the best robe and put it on him. Put a ring on his finger and sandals on his feet. Bring the fattened calf and kill it. Let's have a feast and celebrate. For this son of mine was dead and is alive again; he was lost and is found.' So they began to celebrate" (Luke 15:21-24).

Notice that the father doesn't even let the younger son finish his planned speech. When the prodigal son tells him he is not worthy to be called his father's son and is about to tell him to make him like one of his slaves, the father interrupts him with sentiments of total acceptance, offering symbols of sonship and calling him "son."

That's what the Father of mercy does. He doesn't even let us finish our sentence when we are talking about coming to him as a servant. He shatters our mindsets of slavery with the power of extravagant love and calls us his children.

The second part of the story, however, the part I have often overlooked, focuses on the older brother. Let's read on:

> Meanwhile, the older son was in the field. When he came near the house, he heard music and dancing. So he called one of the servants and asked him what was going on. "Your brother has come," he replied, "and your father has killed the fattened calf because he has him back safe and sound."

> The older brother became angry and refused to go in. So his father went out and pleaded with him. But he answered his father, "Look! All these years I've been slaving for you and never disobeyed your orders. Yet you never gave me even a young goat so I could celebrate with my friends. But when this son of yours who has squandered your property with prostitutes comes home, you kill the fattened calf for him!" [See! The older brother even rivals me with his pity party skills!]

> "My son," the father said, "you are always with me, and everything I have is yours. But we had to celebrate and be glad, because this brother of yours was dead and is alive again" (Luke 15:25-31).

I have read the story of the prodigal son many, many times. I've heard dozens of sermons on it. I've written songs about it. It is one of my favorite stories in the Bible. But at the same time, I have often had a hard time relating to the young son.

You see, I've been pretty good most of my life. I haven't run away from my Father's house, nor have I squandered my inheritance. As someone who is waiting to get married to have sex, I certainly haven't had much loose living. I have lived in my Father's warm home since I became a Christian at sixteen years old. I've loved living here. I've never really wanted to run away.

But after my counseling session, I realized that, though it was hard for me to relate to the younger son, I could deeply identify with the older son. Like him, I have been bitter at God for not giving me what I wanted when I worked so hard for him.

In the parable, the older son stays in his father's house throughout his brother's rebellion. He works the fields for his father. He acts more like a slave than a son.

As I contemplated the story from the perspective of the older brother, I suddenly saw the passage as if it were a movie.

I saw the father, after his younger son ran away, grieving the loss of this son and longing for comfort and connection with his older son. However, the older son slaves away in the fields day after day. After a hard day of work, the eldest son comes home for dinner, sits at the far end of the table, and barely talks to the father. The father wants to talk to him, but the son refuses. He passes his father in the hallway and the father longs to hold him, but the son just brushes past and goes to his room, wallowing in his self-made prison. All he can do is think about what he does for his father, how hard he works, and how his father does not give him enough. He does not believe that his father is a good father.

Then, the prodigal son comes home. But when this joyous occasion takes place, the older son is working in the fields. He misses the homecoming, the running, the laughing and crying, and he misses the party. His work has separated him from the intimate workings of his family, from the celebration of their life together. Even when he finally gets to the party he refuses to go in. He throws his own party of pity, so he misses the party of joy.

When he finally gets to talk to the father about his anger at the situation, he says something to this effect: "I have slaved for you all these years. I have given you everything. But you have not given me anything. Nothing."

I have acted like this older son. I have wondered why, when I have served my Father my whole life, he has not answered my most consistent prayer: the prayer for a family. Forget this whole grace thing. I want God to see my good works and reward me for them.

Sometimes, in the deepest places of my soul, I do much more than throw a pity party. I become bitter. I start to wonder if my Father is really a good father.

As Henri Nouwen says: "Returning home from a lustful escapade seems so much easier than returning home from a cold anger that has rooted itself in the deepest corners of my being. My resentment is not something that can be easily distinguished and dealt with rationally. It is far more pernicious: something that has attached itself to the underside of my virtue."[1]

Nouwen is right. It is difficult to come home to the Father when I consistently allow this cold anger to live inside me, when I consistently allow thoughts like, "I have tried every day of my life to live for you. I have given up a lot to do so. Why, then, am I still not married? Why would you throw other people a party and forget me when I have been faithful to you for so many years? Are you even the good God that you say you are?"

Here is the real question I need to ask myself: Is God not good, or is my perspective not good?

Look at this story. The father is the very definition of a good father. And yet both sons feel like the only way they can be loved is to be his slave.

This good, good father never wanted slaves. He wanted sons. When he addressed each one of them, he specifically called them both sons. In both the case of the rebellious son and the case of the religious son, the father wants to run to them, crying out, "My child. My child! You've come home to me!" He wants to lavish his love on them, spinning them around until they are dizzy with his love, falling down with them, laughing. He wants to cover them with accepting kisses and celebrate their return. Whether they have been living off scraps from a pigsty or living off grimy, bitter thoughts, he wants to give them a loving home to come to at the end of a long, hard journey.

Now and forever, everything he has is theirs. They don't have to steal his inheritance. They don't have to slave for his inheritance. They already have it. This is not the picture of a bad father. It is a picture of the most loving father who ever lived. The father's heart was never wrong. The sons' perspectives were wrong.

My perspective is wrong. My anxiety proves it.

The other day, after listening to me pour out my troubles, a mentor of mine said to me, "Kate, I want you to focus on trusting God during the next few months."

I sounded like a recovering Pharisee when I said, "But I do trust God!" She answered very gently, "No, Kate. No, you don't."

I realized almost automatically that she was right. The fear-ridden frustration I had just spilled out to her indicated how little I trusted him. When it comes down to it, I don't always see him as good. In my heart, I often don't believe that God will give me a good life. Sometimes I believe that even if he is good, I will negate his blessings if I do the wrong thing.

This, my friends, is the life of a slave. This is the life of someone who does not trust her Father.

If I were to tear through these cobwebs of disbelief and really listen to my Father speak to me, he would respond in the same way he responded to the older son.

"My child," he would say, "all that I have is yours. You think that I am withholding from you. If I could lift up the veil of your limited perception, you would know what a good Father I am. You would know there is nothing I have that doesn't belong to you."

And I know what you're thinking because I've had similar thoughts: "Okay, Kate. You say God is good and everything he has is mine. But there is one thing you have overlooked. I still don't have a family."

I know. I don't totally get it either. But I am learning slowly that I don't just want the Lord's loot. I want his love. I don't want to go to God just because I want something. I want to go to him because I love being with him.

One of my favorite Psalms says, "I have stilled and quieted my soul; like a weaned child with its mother. Like a weaned child is my soul within me" (Psalm 131:2). A weaned child doesn't come to its mother for milk anymore. The child comes because she loves being with her mother. She chooses to be still and quiet in her mother's arms. In that moment, she doesn't need anything but her mother's embrace.

I don't understand why I'm not married. I don't understand why there is poverty or slavery in the world. You may not understand your divorce or your being fired or your being sick. You may not understand the disappointments in your life. We may never understand those things in our lifetimes.

But I want to choose to still and quiet my soul. I want to choose to go to my Father even when I don't have answers to my questions. Even when, in my limited perception, I think he is holding out on me. I need to let go of trying to figure it out and I need to rest.

Henri Nouwen says, "I am beginning now to see how radically the character of my spiritual journey will change when I no longer think of God as hiding out (or holding out) and making it as difficult as possible to find him, but instead, as the one looking for me while I am doing the hiding. When I look through God's eyes at my lost self and discover God's joy at my coming home, then my life may become less anguished and more trusting."[2]

The Father reaches out to us. He says, "I never asked you to be a slave. All I ever wanted was for you to be my child. I have been looking for you for a long time. You don't have to hide behind your good deeds, behind your broken dreams, behind your bitterness. Come, eat at my table. When you pass me in the hallway of our house, let me give you a hug. Come rest here in my arms. All I have is yours. My peace is yours. My hope is yours. My passion is yours. My friendship is yours. My heart is yours. My kingdom is yours. My family is yours. Most of all, my love is yours. You have it now. You will never lose it. You just have to believe that it's there."

The cover of my last album is very special to me. It is a drawn picture of a girl who looks like me. She is in a shabby room. She is wearing rags. She is looking into a mirror. In the mirror is an image of the same girl, but she is dressed in a gold and purple robe. There is a beautiful light surrounding her and flowers at her feet. She reaches her hand towards the poor version of herself on the other side of the mirror, a look of compassion and love on her face.

Often people miss this little detail, but on the wall, there is a small framed picture. It is a picture of the same girl in her rags, running toward a man in a purple and gold robe.

Her father.

This picture beautifully depicts that the homecoming of the prodigal son (or the prodigal daughter) is not the end of the story. If we let our Father embrace us, the memory of him running to welcome us with open arms will stay with us forever. It is a picture we will frame and hang on our walls. It will become one of our most precious possessions, whether we are staying in a palace or in a dingy, tiny room.

After we have been embraced by God, when we look in the mirror, we will not see someone in rags, bitter and torn. We will see ourselves as the Father sees us. Beautiful. Compassionate toward ourselves and others. We will see ourselves wearing his robe, wearing his identity. We will no longer be slaves but beloved children.

The way we see God will change everything, even the way we see ourselves.

I realize now that pity parties are all right every once in a while because they allow me to express my pain, but God wants to throw me a much greater party. A life-changing party. One that makes my thoughts of bitterness fall to the wayside. One in which my Father clothes me with the robe of his mercy, the cloak of his joy. One in which I am the honored guest.

A party that celebrates that I have come home to him.

Kate's Corner of Wisdom
How to Live Life Well

1. Love God.
2. Love the person standing in front of you…even if you're looking in a mirror.

How to Build Your Own Family, Part 1: Giving Yourself to Others

When I tell people I am writing a book about being a single Christian, I inevitably get into conversations with them about relationships. If they are also single Christians, we usually end up telling our sob stories and our success stories. We share our fears about getting older and our frustrations with not having a family. We comment about how it seems like Christian guys would rather clean every bathroom in Grand Central Station with a toothbrush than ask us out on a date because of the pressure they feel to get married too fast.

Et cetera, et cetera, et cetera.

Even when I am not talking to other people about my love life or lack thereof, I am infinitely more aware of it than usual because I have had my heart broken pretty badly this season. I have been saturated with thoughts about my own loneliness. And now, after months of thinking about it, I am not just lovesick, I am sick of love. Of thinking about love. Of talking about love. Of reading about love. Of writing about love. Most of all, I am sick of thinking about myself.

In the book *Singled Out*, John Stott says, "The greatest danger [singles] face is self-centeredness. We may live alone and have total freedom to plan our own schedule, with nobody else to modify it or even give us advice. If we are not careful, we may find the whole world revolving around ourselves."[1]

In other words, as singles, it's really easy for us to become self-absorbed. In fact, I have become really self-absorbed.

It is in selfish seasons like this that I wrongfully believe I have no choice over whether I have a family or not. While it is true that I can't get a husband the same way I can get a degree, I do have some control. The catch is, what I can have at this point is not the husband-and-kids-and-white-picket-fence family that I expected to have. Instead, I can make the choice to build my own, beautiful nontraditional family. And there is no better way to do this than to put myself in situations in which I can love people who desperately need it.

A good example of this is my friend Jude. Jude grew up as the child of Dutch immigrants. She worked overseas for a season and then, twenty-six years ago, she became a missionary with InnerChange. Each of those twenty-six years was spent in the low-income Latino apartments I mentioned earlier in the book. Jude works among the people in this poor community, and she is also a professor at Fuller Theological Seminary. You don't often imagine professors living in one of the poorest neighborhoods in Los Angeles, but that is the life she has chosen.

Jude realized early in her singleness that she didn't want to pine away for a life she didn't have. She felt like she might want to get married at some point, but she wasn't obsessed with finding her husband. She refused to spend her life waiting, so she dove into an interesting, rich life by sharing the love of Jesus with the poor.

Jude was still single into her late thirties, but she wasn't that worried about it. She didn't feel the aching loneliness many of us struggle with because she had chosen in her twenties to build her own family with the people to whom she ministered. Her brothers and sisters and sons and daughters in this nontraditional family helped fulfill her innate desire to give and receive love.

When Jude was thirty-nine, she unexpectedly met her husband, who was interning with InnerChange. He was African-American and eight years her junior, but they didn't let that get in the way of the love they knew God had for them. They never had any biological children, but they spiritually adopted a Latino boy, Chris, who had grown up in the same apartments the couple lived in.

The daughter of Dutch immigrants marrying an African-American man and adopting Latino children? This was probably not the life Jude expected! But it is so much more colorful and deep a life than she ever imagined.

Like Jude, I want to stop being so self-absorbed in my own season of singleness. I want to remember the lonely and brokenhearted not only because it will make me feel better, but also because God himself commands us to care for the poor and the downtrodden and the abandoned.

A few years ago, I did an exercise that shook me out of my self-absorbed bubble and made me realize how deeply God cares about the poor. I was listening to a teaching on biblical justice by Rob Morris, founder of Love146, an inspiring organization that fights child exploitation. During the teaching, Rob had listeners flip through their Bibles for ten minutes and look for verses about taking care of the poor, helpless, or hurting.

I opened to a Psalm but figured that I should move on to another book, since the Psalms probably wouldn't have much about taking care of the poor. But one of the first verses I read was Psalm 41:1, which says, "Blessed is he who considers the poor; the LORD will deliver him in time of trouble" (NKJV).

I flipped a few more pages, thinking the first one was a fluke. Then I read, "He has given freely to the poor, his righteousness endures forever" and "He raises the poor from the dust and lifts the needy from the ash heap" (Psalm 112:9 NASB and Psalm 113:7). Then, "I know that the LORD secures justice for the poor and upholds the cause of the needy" in Psalm 140:12.

Those were just a few of the many verses I read. By the time the ten minutes had run out, I had come across dozens of verses about helping the poor.

Let's try that same experiment here. Set this book down for a moment and pick up your Bible. Flip through it and, with no help from concordances, mark down all the verses you find about taking care of the poor. Do it for ten minutes. Write down all of the references. After the ten minutes are up, ponder what you read for a while, breathing deep and listening to God's heart.

_____

_____

_____

_____

_____

_____

_____

_____

_____

_____

_____

_____

_____

What kind of verses did you find? Was it easy to find them? My bet is that they were everywhere you looked. Those verses are all over the Bible—there are around two thousand of them.

Since I did that exercise, I am constantly noticing verses about taking care of the poor. I couldn't believe I hadn't seen them before. I mean, I knew that Jesus talked about the poor, but not like this. I didn't see that it was on his mind all the time, that loving the poor and those who have no family was one of the passions of his life.

If the God I love talks about this topic so many times, shouldn't I make it a focus of my life as well? Shouldn't I care about it because he cares about it? I don't want to be like Thomas Jefferson, who cut out every verse of the Bible he didn't like and glued all the other passages together. I don't want to pick and choose the parts of the Bible that will convince me the world revolves around me and my pain.

Understanding how much Jesus loved the poor was what drove me to work with traveling street youth. I loved sitting across the table from my homeless friends, laughing and crying with them as if we had been companions for years. I loved going to the music class I taught and talking to Star, with his toothless grin and his six-foot-five hugs that immersed me in love. He cried when I sang and would say, "I don't understand why I do that. Why do I cry every time you sing?"

I loved having Roach tell me his life story before I recorded one of his rap songs, I loved seeing him weep uncontrollably when we prayed for him, and I loved hearing him tell my teammate, "You're the best friend I have in this city."

I loved receiving e-mail messages from Jack, my favorite street friend, who recently turned himself in to the police and served a stint in prison because he was getting serious about walking with God and he felt like turning himself in was the right thing to do. The morning of my writing this chapter, I found this in my inbox: "If no one has told you they love you today, give me a call. Because I will tell you." I need someone in my family to tell me that sometimes.

The fact that it is a street friend who tells me that, someone who seems so different from me, makes it all the more beautiful.

When I walk side by side with people this way, I glimpse what it would be like to build my own nontraditional family. Father Gregory Boyle, who places recovering gang members in jobs, says this in his beautiful book *Tattoos on the Heart*.

> Soon we imagine, with God, this circle of compassion. Then we imagine no one standing outside that circle, moving ourselves closer to the margins so that the margins themselves will be erased. We stand there with those whose dignity has been denied. We locate ourselves with the poor and the powerless and voiceless. At the edges, we join the easily despised and readily left out. We stand with the demonized so that the demonizing will stop. We situate ourselves right next to the disposable so that the day will come when we stop throwing people away…And so the voices at the margins get heard and the circle of compassion widens.[2]

As Mother Teresa put it, "If we have no peace, it is because we have forgotten we belong to each other."[3] Let's remember that we belong to each other. Let's love other people enough to remind them that we belong to each other. Maybe then we would finally have some peace, even if we don't have the traditional family we always wanted.

I know there are a million causes that want your resources. A million different ministries vying for your attention. It can be overwhelming to hear all the statistics. Sometimes you don't know where to look. You don't know if you can make a difference, so you don't look anywhere. You look away.

But behind these causes are real people with real faces and real voices and real senses of humor and real tears. People like the girls in Love146's safe homes. People like Jack. People that you can really help. People that can really help you.

If you don't think that your one voice can make a difference, consider my friend Samson, whom I worked alongside on a trip to India. When Samson was born, his father heard a voice saying he should sacrifice his son to a Hindu goddess. He said, "No. That will never happen." That very same day, Samson was struck with a mysterious illness. He was sick for four months. His parents took him to hospitals and witch doctors, but no treatment worked. He was so sick his family was sure he would die. But one day, a woman came and prayed for him fervently. He got better almost immediately afterward. It was clear even from an early age that Samson had something important to do in life. A few years later, the father died in a monsoon. Samson's mother and her six children had to go to begging in the streets. She had no choice but to allow Samson to become a slave at only eight years old.

The very day that Samson was to leave the family, a member of Compassion International came to Samson's mother to tell her that Samson had been chosen as a Compassion child. This means that someone in the States would give a monthly gift to their family. Samson no longer had to go into slavery. Not only that, the monthly gift allowed his entire family to live in a house, get food, and receive a Christian education. His family accepted Christ, and they helped lead the entire Hindu village to the Lord. Samson grew up to start Peace Gospel, a ministry that takes care of orphans, widows, and lepers (www.peacegospel.org).

I went to visit Samson's village while I was there. His childhood home was a simple hut with dirt floors. The only thing on the wall was a framed picture of his father, along with a tiny picture of the Compassion International sponsor. One of the few possessions the family had was an album filled with letters from their sponsor.

I looked at that picture and letters and thought, *I wonder if this guy has any clue how his small monthly sacrifice changed the life of a little boy, his village, and the lives of countless widows and orphans in Samson's organization.*

My advice for you is to believe your voice can make a difference.

Learn about your cause. Read books on it. Introduce yourself to the people behind it. Find out what you and your friends can do to make a difference. Don't just serve at a soup kitchen; come out from the serving line and sit and eat with the precious people you have served. Don't just give money to an organization that fights child exploitation; find out how to write to the kids in the safe home and get to know them. Shane Claiborne says in his book *The Irresistible Revolution*, "What our world is desperately in need of [is] lovers, people who are building deep, genuine relationships with fellow strugglers along the way, and who actually know the faces of the people behind the issues they are concerned about."[4]

Like the note Fred Rogers carried that said, "Frankly, there isn't anyone you couldn't learn to love once you've heard their story," we know that hearing people's stories makes them become human to us. Somehow, recognizing the trials that person has overcome allows you to see how beautiful and strong they are. Can you imagine what the world would be like if all of us set out to find someone very different from us and then learned their stories? To seek to understand them rather than to judge them? Again from Father Gregory Boyle: "Here is what we seek: a compassion that can stand in awe at what the poor have to carry rather than stand in judgment at how they carry it."[5]

When you become friends with people who are hurting, they almost always end up bringing beauty to your life that you never expected. You realize that we all want the same thing: family.

Getting to know people changes your priorities. You would rather comfort them and be comforted by them than saturate your own life with comforts that are not attached to human beings, or to be saturated by your own disappointments. If all you think about is love and your lack of it, try to gather up the courage to walk out the door into a world that can be cold, a world that might have pain in it. But a world that is beautiful. A world where you will truly be alive. A world where you might even find a family.

Finally, let's look at love through the eyes of two very different men: Buddha and Jesus.

As Frederick Buechner says,

> Buddha sits enthroned beneath the Bo tree in the lotus position. His lips are faintly parted in the smile of one who has passed beyond every power in earth or heaven to touch him. "He who loves fifty has fifty woes, he who loves ten has ten woes, he who loves none has no woes," he has said. His eyes are closed. Christ, on the other hand, stands in the garden of Gethsemane, angular, beleaguered. His face is lost in shadows so that you can't even see his lips, and before all the powers in earth or heaven he is powerless. "This is my commandment, that you love one another as I have loved you."[6]

Buddha says that if you don't love as many people, you won't have as much pain. And he's probably right. It's hard to love people. The reward of self-absorption is that you will be very comfortable. But you will also be very alone.

Jesus, on the other hand, says to love, love, love, love, no matter how hard it is, no matter what you have to give up. He tells us to passionately love, as he has passionately loved us. Passionately love our friends, our spouse, our children, our enemies, the poor.

Love even if we have to die for it. Because that is what he did.

Jesus was never absorbed by himself. He was never absorbed with avoiding pain. He was always absorbed by his desire to love.

How to Build Your Own Family, Part 2: Living in Community

When I was going to be in ministry school for a season, a friend arranged for me to live on a farm with four other single girls. I had never met the girls before, and I had butterflies in my stomach when I drove onto Shiloh Farm that first day.

Soon after introducing themselves to me, my four new housemates said, "We are doing something this weekend, but you don't have to join us if you don't want to."

I said, "No, I'd love to join you!"

They said, "Well, you really don't have to join us."

And I said, "No, I'd love to!"

And then they said, "We're slaughtering chickens."

"I'm in," I said.

I figured that if I were going to be eating those chickens, I should at least help get them to my plate. I won't get into the grisly details about that weekend, but let's just say that we had farm-fresh organic chicken for dinner a lot that year and I now know how to use a machete.

We knew the chickens would taste wonderful in all of their organic, nongenetically modified glory, but their little bird legs were spread out in a way that made it obvious they did not come from the store. We stuffed the chickens for flavor, and, with their sprawled-out legs, the poor chickens looked like they were giving birth to lemons.

I got to know some unique animal friends while I lived there on the farm. There was the chicken I liked to call Pet Cemetery. She had somehow hurt her neck and her head was turned almost completely around to face behind her. As a result, she slowly walked backward instead of forward. It was totally creepy.

We also had Peg Leg, a rooster that had lost his leg when a horse stepped on it. My roommate Kristy fastened a popsicle-stick prosthetic onto the nub, but it didn't help. Peg Leg just figured out how to get around on one leg. I frequently saw him hopping around the farm. He was definitely the ladies' man of the farm despite his disability. I now understand the term "cocky" in a whole new light.

And then there were the bunnies. We tried hard to decide what to do about our rabbit problem. The rabbits were nuisances. They destroyed our garden, so we knew we needed to find a way to get them off the farm. When we found a bunch of tiny babies in our toolshed, we figured out exactly what to do: We brought them into the house and let them hop all over our beds and sleep with us because they were so cute.

Captain Jack Sparrow became one of our favorite bunnies. He was black with white spots. My four-year-old nephew John Mark would visit and loved feeding carrots to that little bunny. To this day, every time I visit John Mark he asks me where Captain Jack is. I tell him that he got married, moved to Los Angeles, and became an accountant with a nice mustache.

People would often ask me if someone else ran the farm, having a hard time believing that a group of girls would want to do that. But those four were very unique girls.

The four friends had moved out to California together from Cairo, Illinois. In Cairo, they had all met at a prayer ministry in a very poor, ninety-percent African-American community, and eventually they decided to go to California for school. When I moved in with them, I soon learned that they were intentional about community. We shared all our food. No permanent marker labeling was allowed. People often think that sharing food is a strange thing to do in a roommate situation, but isn't sharing food what a family does? I didn't have as much money as the other girls during that season, so I couldn't contribute as much as they did. They didn't care. They didn't keep tabs.

Every weeknight one of us would cook dinner for everyone else. Even if we didn't have time, we made time to do it. We sat down at the table and talked about our days. Afterward we would often sit in the living room and talk more, processing our hopes and disappointments and dreams. There was always a lot of laughter and love in that house.

It ended up being a very hard year for me, with a breakup and a major struggle with depression. I was so thankful to have the girls on the farm around me during that season. The longer I was there, the more I realized why I loved living with them so much: Even if they were not a traditional family, they were a family, and they allowed me to be a part of it.

One of the girls, Kristy, was forty-two—a bit older than the others. I often talked to her when I needed wisdom, and she always had some to offer. A month or so after I moved in, I asked her if it was hard for her to be unmarried and with no children at her age. That's when she let me know for the first time that she felt called to a life of celibacy. She wanted to be devoted to the Lord and to loving the people around her without being married, and she was totally at peace with that.

During our conversation, Kristy said something that I have thought about quite a bit since then. She said, "Even though I've been called to a life of singleness, I know that I don't want to be alone. I know that I will choose to live in intentional community for the rest of my life."

I learned that she was the one who started the prayer house in

Cairo. The intentionality of that community was no mistake. She valued community, and so she worked hard to create an environment that worked toward that goal. With the help of her friends, she had not only built a ministry, she had also built a family.

(On a side note, one day I was talking to a classmate who had a male friend in his forties who also felt called to celibacy. Without even thinking about it, I said, "Oh, my gosh! I have a roommate named Kristy who is also in her forties and celibate and she is wonderful! We should set them up on a date!" My friend looked at me as if I were crazy, and I realized I had just said one of the most ironic things ever.)

When I moved back to Boulder a year later, I lived in a more typical roommate situation with five girls in the house. I got along fine with my roommates but we didn't see a lot of each other. We had different schedules and were hardly at the house at the same time, except to sleep. Even though we shared a kitchen, we barely ever ate meals together. I would lie in bed at night and marvel at the fact that there were a few girls under the same roof as me that I barely knew. In other words, it was like most roommate situations in America.

After two years of this, I knew something had to change. I was too lonely. I found another farm in the city called Jacob's Springs, where six adults and four kids live together in intentional community. I live in a great big white farmhouse that is full of laughter and crying and conversation. It is probably a bit messier than it would be if I lived alone. I often eat livers and hearts because we have a whole freezer full of them that don't get sold. I have to step around kids' toys to take a shower. I have to have difficult conversations every once in a while. For one glorious day we had a baby raccoon living in our oven.

And I love every moment of it. So many fewer comforts, but so much more love. Like Kristy, I am learning that if I am single I need to look for intentional community wherever I am and then sacrifice to be a part of that family. If my circumstances haven't handed me a traditional family, I am going to work to find family anyway.

You have to do a little searching to find communities like Shiloh Farm and Jacob's Springs, and there is a good reason for this. It isn't that comfortable to live in community. It takes work, it takes time, and it takes vulnerability. The pursuit of happiness is written right into our country's Declaration of Independence, and the default attitude tends to be to live as comfortably as possible. And so without even meaning to we end up sacrificing community for convenience.

When I went to Italy the first time, I was struck by how essential their family life was to their happiness. The whole country is not run by love of money or technology or entertainment; it is centered on and rooted in family. I started taking notice of what they did in order to foster a culture that values community so much. The two things that struck me the most were that the Italians ate meals together (mostly at home) every day around a table, and that even if they owned cars they would often take time out of their day to walk places. The people in the village I was in understood that eating meals together and walking through their community were too important to give up, no matter how busy life became. They knew that conversations happen around tables and on street corners and around food that takes time and effort to cook. The people understood that slowing down to eat and to walk does not just nurture the body, but that it also nurtures connection. It brings about family.

Connection does not happen so much when you are eating frozen dinners in front of the TV. But at least we are comfortable there, right?

From my experience, this is the world most Americans have created to keep ourselves as comfortable as possible: We wake up and turn on the radio so we don't have to think. We eat our cereal alone so we don't have to cook. We drive to our jobs so we don't have to interact. We nod to our roommates when we get home so we don't have to invest. We put up fences so we don't have to connect. We do social networking so we don't have to communicate anything deep.

We check our iPhones and laptops as often as possible to saturate our minds with information so we don't have to contemplate. We watch our televisions so we don't have to feel. And in these days that blur into months that blur into lifetimes, we are comfortable. But we are also unhappy and lonely.

In *The Intentional Christian Community Handbook*, David Janzen discusses the idea that the convenient invention of the car changed the community life of America forever. He writes,

> This American life is a life dispersed: we work ten miles away with people who live twenty miles beyond that, buy food grown a thousand miles away from grocery clerks who live in a different subdivision, date people from the other side of town, and worship with people who live an hour's drive from one another...There is little sense of consonance, commitment, spontaneity, or stability in this paved new world. Because there is so little over-lap in our different spheres of life, there is little chance for our socializing, creativity, or service to be spontane-ous. The nearest things to spontaneous occasions in the fragmented lifestyle of suburbia is the persistent stream of texts, tweets, and status updates on our cell phones.[1]

We are part of a society that has often traded in community for comfort and we should be aware of the consequences of that trade. If we want to foster community, we are going to have to make a conscious effort to go against the flow of our fast-moving and con-venient environment. We are going to have to give up some of our comfort in order to create a space for love.

How do we do this? By taking time in our days to eat with people, even if doing so is inconvenient. By planting a community garden that our neighbors can share. By stopping by a friend's house to bring them a gift. Small things make a big difference. But what is, in my opinion, the best way to go against the flow of our nonspontaneous culture? Create an intentional community in which you live with other people in order to foster family life.

One of my favorite films in which the character discovers the joy of living in community is *The Visitor*. In it, the main character—an older man named Walter—lives in a house alone in Connecticut. He hates his job as a professor. His wife, who was a classical pianist, died, so we find him taking piano lessons in order to remember her and fill his empty days. But he doesn't enjoy it.

Walter owns another apartment in Manhattan. When he visits his apartment on a business trip, he is surprised and furious to find that there are two illegal immigrants, Tarek and Zainab, living in his second home. The immigrant couple had not meant to steal Walter's home; they rented the apartment from a swindler who pretended to own the apartment.

At first, Walter is angry and demands that the couple leave his apartment. But he is convinced to let them stay there for a while, and slowly he and the couple develop a close friendship. Walter learns to play hand drums from Tarek. In one of my favorite scenes, Walter, a straight-laced businessman, runs from his office during his lunch hour to join a drum circle with Tarek at the local park. There is such joy on his face as he plays drums in his business suit. Indeed, through his relationship with the immigrant couple, Walter discovers who he is and what he loves.

After many months of the three of them living together, the couple faces the threat of deportation, and Walter fights hard to keep them in the United States. You can see how much he loves them; they have now become the family that he longed for.

We would do well to follow in Walter's footsteps. We would do well to move beyond our lonely, convenient lives in order to build our own families. I would love to see a movement of singles who are committed to having a family even if they are still looking for a spouse or if they have decided to remain single. Maybe these singles might even choose to live together, make meals together, dream together, like the people at Shiloh Farm and Jacob Springs.

You can be in a family if you want to be. You don't have to be alone. You can build your own family. Certainly, living in intentional community takes commitment and letting go of some things you love—like some of your independence, like making sure there is not a spot on the countertop, like having to talk to and listen to people you may not always like, like taking the time to eat and laugh and share life together, like pulling yourself away from your Facebook page. It might take you having a vision and sacrificing to make it happen.

Personally, I would rather have covenant than independence. I'd rather make meals that take time and effort with my friends than eat a bowl of cereal, go to my room, and watch YouTube videos alone. I'd rather have a house that is full of love and companionship with a few dirty dishes in the sink than a perfectly ordered, spotless house with no one in it.

I'd rather have family.

It's not good for us to be alone. No matter how much freedom we have when we are alone, it is not good. God himself said that.

It is good for us to be in a family, even if we have to build our own.

Thirty, Flirty, and Fertile

When I lived at Shiloh Farm, my roommates (all of whom are over thirty and single) and I went to a 90s-themed roller skating party. At first we couldn't think what to wear, so we decided to look online for inspiration. As we glanced over the images that were a result of our search, many bad fashion memories came back to us. The Jennifer Aniston haircut. The little plastic circle that you could slip onto your T-shirt to make it almost look like you tied it, but not quite. The hat with the big sunflower on top that could have come right off the show *Blossom*.

My roommate Amanda decided to play the part of the early 90s girl. She was quite *Saved by the Bell*-esque, wearing florescent clothes with funny patterns and overly-teased bangs. My other roommate, Jess, decided to go for the mid-90s grunge look, complete with a morose spirit hanging over her that was obviously inspired by Pearl Jam. Jess dressed the part perfectly: cotton leggings, Converse, and an oversized flannel shirt. But the little detail that pulled it all together was a black velvet ribbon choker with a cross hanging from it. Jess parted her bangs down the middle, put some black makeup around her eyes, and wore frosted lip gloss. When cheery early-90s

Amanda saw gloomy mid-90s Jess, she tried to enlighten her. She said, "Jesus can lift your spirits AND your hair!"

At first I was amused when I saw Jess's outfit. It looked just like what I wore almost every day when I was in college.

Then I got a little freaked out.

THAT LOOKS JUST LIKE WHAT I WORE ALMOST EVERY DAY WHEN I WAS IN COLLEGE!

What? How could this be? How could I be having flashbacks of my high school and college days while getting ready for a decade theme party?

I started counting backward. It's been twenty years since the early 90s. TWENTY YEARS? I remember my mom going to a "Remember the 60s" party when I was growing up. And now that was me! The 60s are twenty years from the 80s, and now the 90s are twenty years from today. Is it possible?

I had to sit down on the bed for a moment to calm myself down. Then I put on my florescent orange shirt and big black boots, applied a ridiculous amount of hairspray, and headed off to the party.

I got even more freaked out once we got there.

This roller skating joint had not been redone since the very decade we were celebrating. Or if it had been, it had been redecorated to look like every single roller skating place I ever went to when I was in middle school. Orange carpet. Disco balls and lights that put patterns on the dance floor. Brown roller skates with dangerously long orange shoelaces. (Doesn't anyone even test those roller skates? There are children wearing these things, for heaven's sake!) People going at very high speeds who suddenly swerve around the gateway on the verge of crashing, flashing a smile at you to cover up the fact that they were about to knock six people over. Couples holding hands. Awkward people inching very slowly along the walls, trying to pretend they have some semblance of balance. The inevitable game of Crack the Whip, where a line of people hold hands while skating around the circle, forgetting the unfortunate people at the end of the line who are going so fast they could at any moment be propelled against the wall.

When I ventured onto the rink, I wondered if anyone was watching me. I was quite cognizant of the way I smoothly ran my wheels across the floor, of how hot I looked in my one-sleeved shirt, of how all the 25-year-old guys there probably had no idea that I was in high school in the 90s because I still looked so young and vivacious. But those thoughts all stopped abruptly when my too-long shoelaces got caught up in my wheels and I fell flat on my face.

Just like in middle school.

It was as if I were at this party in the past and the present at the same time. It was tripping me out almost as much as my too-long shoelaces were tripping me up.

After I brushed myself off and started another lap, my ears tuned in to the music that was playing.

Even. More. Freaked. Out.

I know "Ice Ice Baby" was from the 90s. It seems like it belongs in the 90s. The same goes for MC Hammer and "U Can't Touch This." But what about "Mr. Jones" by Counting Crows? "Semi-Charmed Life"? "One Headlight" by The Wallflowers? It does not seem like fifteen-plus years since I first heard those songs.

I came home from that party feeling pretty old.

People say to me all the time, "Well, age doesn't matter. It's just a number."

You know what my response always is?

"Tell that to my uterus."

My uterus and I have had quite a few problems in our relationship as of late. In truth, my uterus is pretty frustrated with me.

The argument she has with me all the time sounds like this: "Kate, what am I good for if I don't house a little baby for nine months? I've been sitting down here for thirty-some years with nothing to do! I need a job, Kate! Go out there! Find yourself a man! Get married and get these eggs fertilized."

I feel sheepish and guilty every time my uterus and I talk. Because she's right. I do need to "get out there." But it's more complicated than it seems. I try to tell her that, and she says, "Why didn't you go out with all those guys who liked you ten years ago? Why were you so picky?"

"I don't know, Uterus. Life only makes sense in the rearview mirror." That's what I always say. Or maybe that's a country song. Either way, it's true.

According to the social norms, my uterus and I only have a few years to get ourselves pregnant.

Because the very day that I turn the dreaded number forty, my eggs will shrivel up and die. Forever. If they do—by some monumental miracle of God—get fertilized after that day, my babies will supposedly look like a cross between Jay Leno and Steven Tyler.

At least that's what I'm told.

If you look at these quotes from some of the aforementioned chick flicks that have now been emblazoned in my head for many, many years, you'll understand better what I'm talking about.

In *When Harry Met Sally*, Sally is thinking about the fact that she is still unmarried while talking to her friend Harry, and exclaims, "And I'm gonna be forty!"

"When?" Harry responds.

"Someday!"

"In eight years!" Harry says.

And here's the clincher from Sally—the thing that reveals her fears: "But it's there! It's just sitting there like this big dead end."

A big dead end. Not the most positive picture of midlife painted by our darling Meg Ryan.

In *Bridget Jones's Diary*, Bridget Jones is asked why there are so many single women in their thirties. She responds, "I guess it doesn't help that we have scales under our clothes."

In *Sleepless in Seattle*, a friend says to Meg Ryan's character, "It's easier to get killed by a terrorist than to find a husband after the age of forty."

Meg responds indignantly, and her friend retorts, "That's right; it's not true. But it feels true."

When we look at the messages in these movies, I wonder if we have valid reasons to be afraid of hitting middle age without a family or if we just live in a culture that is freaked out by the number forty. What are the facts here?

The notion of a woman having a greater chance of getting killed by a terrorist than to marry after forty has been debunked. This false picture stemmed from an article which declared that single women over thirty had only a five-percent chance of marrying, and that after the age of forty they only had a two-percent chance left (which is still a much higher percentage than getting killed by a terrorist). Looking at the US census bureau for that year (which was in the mid-80s), those percentages proved to be quite different: Women who were over thirty had a sixty-six-percent chance of still getting married and women over forty still had a twenty-three-percent chance of getting married.

And yet the picture of terrorists being more numerous than husbands was still emblazoned into our anti-forty media. That false statistic found its way into the TV show *Frasier* and the movies *The Holiday, Addicted to His Love*, and *Sleepless in Seattle*. It's almost like America thinks it's funny to freak us single thirty-somethings out.

We get the same kind of sense of impending doom when it comes to having babies after the magic number forty. Although there are admittedly greater risks, women can have perfectly healthy babies at an older age. Plenty of celebrities have had babies over forty: Jane Seymour, Emma Thompson, Susan Sarandon, Madonna, Cheryl Tiegs (twins at fifty-two!), J.K. Rowling, Geena Davis, Meryl Streep, Helen Hunt, Halle Berry, Nicole Kidman, Mariah Carey...shall I go on?

Friends of mine who are midwives have told me that they have had many clients in their forties—and even fifties—who have had healthy children. One of my midwife friends in Portland says the majority of her clients are over forty.

And if an older woman cannot or does not want to have biological children, she can choose to adopt. I have always wanted to adopt. Even when I was in college, I would tell people that if I found out I couldn't have children, I would simply take in a child who didn't have a home. I don't think I would be devastated if I found out I could not have children of my own. There are plenty of children who desperately need a loving family, and I would love to give it to them. I have even considered adopting as a single woman if I get into my forties and am still not married.

Every time I see adoptive families, I feel so drawn to them that I figure my longing must be a stirring from the Lord. Every time I watch a movie about a teacher reaching out to hurting teenagers—especially in the inner city—it is inevitable that I cry through the whole movie. I don't know if that means I will adopt inner-city kids or if I will just work in the inner city loving them. But I do know that either way, I want to be a big part of these children's lives. I want to love them well.

"Okay, Kate," you say. "You've made a good argument. Maybe it's not as bad as I thought to have babies or to adopt after forty. But I don't want to be in a wheelchair and on oxygen when my kid graduates high school."

I know. I feel the same way. But I also want to wish away the fact that "Only Wanna Be With You" by Hootie and the Blowfish came out in 1995. I don't like getting older, but I am getting older. I can choose to be angry at my reality, or I can choose to accept it and make the best of it.

There you have it. All the great arguments that I have for you and that I tell my own heart on a regular basis. *Just ignore the culture and pretend you are young. Just adopt. Just accept reality.* I have my author hat on right now, so it would be easy to give you those answers and leave it at that. But I don't want to do that. You know why? Because I don't want us to be alone. We need each other. So I'm going to take the hat off now and admit that when it comes to the thought of never having a family, I am just as scared as you are. Really, really scared. I joke about my uterus and about roller skating parties, but when I can't sleep at night I am probably lying awake thinking that I am getting older and might never do all the things I dream of doing, especially having a family.

There are things I love about getting older. I feel comfortable in my own skin. I have overcome a lot and have become a much wiser human being. I can make strong decisions, I communicate well with the people I care about, and I love who I am, all of which were distant desires a decade ago.

But there are other things I hate about getting older. I cringe when people ask me how old I am, especially men I am attracted to. After I read that even older men look for women under thirty-five, I have seriously considered faking my age on dating websites. Lately I have avoided being around children, simply because it makes me so sad that I might never have my own. I wake up some mornings not wanting to have to go through the day because it means getting older. I have a birthday coming up this weekend. I am forcing myself to celebrate, but really, I want to cry every time I think about it.

At my age, I don't have a lot of choices in my dating life. On the rare occasion I do get to go on a date, my fear often kicks in. I try desperately not to be desperate. If I am not careful, I end up wearing my biological clock on my sleeve. I all but stand up on the table and do an interpretive dance of the old DC Talk song "Time Is Ticking Away," complete with my arms moving to the rhythm like a clock.

My memories are starting to feel further and further away, which really frightens me. I wonder if my life has meant anything. I feel pressure to find more meaning in life because time is slipping away so fast.

So there it is. The honest truth. I am scared to death. And if you get down to it, I am scared of death. Of getting older and dying without doing all that I was supposed to do.

One of my greatest fears is that I'll get older without having a family, and the only way I can possibly get over this fear is to trust God. Yes, I am scared, but I need to believe that if God wants me to have a family, I will have a family. He has no time constraints. Nothing is too difficult for him. On the other hand, if I don't have a family, I will be okay. I can still choose to live a beautiful life.

I refuse to let my belief in the goodness of God rest on whether or not I have a family. There are some things I will never understand and this may be one of them, but I will keep on believing in the goodness of God.

In Ecclesiastes 3:10-11, Solomon gives us these words: "I have seen the burden God has laid on men. He has made everything beautiful in its time. He has also set eternity in the hearts of men; yet they cannot fathom what God has done from beginning to end."

Let's look at this verse a little closer. You read the first part—"I have seen the burden God has laid on man"—and, if you are like me, you wonder, "What is this mysterious burden that God has laid on men? To have to work to provide food and shelter for your family? The evil in the world? Mosquitos? The Kardashian sisters?"

The next sentence identifies the great burden that God has laid on us, and it surprises me. Here is the burden: He makes all things beautiful.

Why would God making something beautiful be a burden? That sounds much more like a blessing, doesn't it?

Read on and you might understand: "He has made everything beautiful in its time." The great burden is not that he makes all things beautiful. It is that he makes all things beautiful in his time, not in our time. In ways that are beyond our limited perception.

Sometimes I get angry at his timing. I do not like getting older. I don't like that our memories of roller skating are getting further and

further away. But I cannot "fathom what God has done from beginning to end." Standing within the walls of time, I don't understand.

Do you know which verses precede the one about God making
all things beautiful? They are very familiar. I'll give you a hint: The
words of the verse may have been played at my mom's "Remember
the 60s" party.

> There is a time for everything, and a season for every
> activity under the heavens:
> a time to be born and a time to die,
> a time to plant and a time to uproot,
> a time to kill and a time to heal,
> a time to tear down and a time to build,
> a time to weep and a time to laugh,
> a time to mourn and a time to dance,
> a time to scatter stones and a time to gather them,
> a time to embrace and a time to refrain from
>   embracing,
> a time to search and a time to give up,
> a time to keep and a time to throw away,
> a time to tear and a time to mend,
> a time to be silent and a time to speak,
> a time to love and a time to hate,
> a time for war and a time for peace
> (Ecclesiastes 3:1-8).

There is a season to everything. A time for everything. Everyone's
story and everyone's rhythm is different. Not one is better than the
other.

My friend Sam said to me the other day, "Kate, do you realize
that if you'd had a child a few years ago, he or she would most likely
have had Lyme disease? Maybe it was not God withholding from
you when he didn't let you have a baby at that age. Maybe it was his
grace. Maybe he wanted to wait for you to be healthy to let you have
a child." It had never occurred to me before that my having to wait

might not have been God stealing something, but him waiting to give me something much better.

We can't often see things clearly from our limited perception. Perhaps God stands above us, above time, as if we were in a parade, and he throws down love on us, like floating ticker tapes. He throws down love from that lofty window, seeing the bigger picture, and we don't understand what he is doing from beginning to end. But the love still falls down on us, surrounding us as we march on, unaware.

Thank you, Jesus. Thank you for your grace. Whether I have a husband or not, whether I have children or not, and even when I don't understand your timing or my disappointments, I can trust this one thing: You make all things beautiful.

The Pheromone Adventures

K ate, I have decided that you are the eighth wonder of the world," said my brother as we ate peanut butter and honey sandwiches at our grandma's house.

"What do you mean?"

"I mean it's a complete mystery why you've had this litany of men who act interested in you and then drop you like you're hot. Or like you're not hot. Errr...You know what I mean. Why is this happening?"

"That's the question I have asked myself for the last twenty years, Will."

"Well, I have a theory," he said mysteriously. "It's your pheromones."

"What about my pheromones?"

"Maybe they're not working right."

"What?" I said, slightly offended. "My pheromones are great! Never been better! I have very sexy pheromones! In fact, my pheromones closely resemble Angelina Jolie's, that's how sexy they are!"

"I'm not so sure," said Will carefully. "Everybody loves you, but nobody wants to marry you. Perhaps there is a reason for that. What if you don't have Angelina Jolie pheromones? What if your pheromones are a little more like the awkward girl at the middle school dance who is afraid someone will get tangled up in her braces if she kisses anyone? I'm not saying that you yourself are awkward, just that those little molecules inside of you might be malfunctioning. Don't let it get you down too much. Maybe those sweet little wallflower pheromones of yours can get a makeover."

I went home, lay in bed, and pondered my brother's observations. What if all these years, all this heartbreak, all these times hearing *Kate, I think you're amazing, but...* and all this wondering if I'm not pretty enough, nice enough, good enough, special enough— what if all this time the only problem was that I don't have the right secreted chemicals to trigger a social response in members of the opposite sex?

I sat up and started researching. One article I read said that when women are given men's shirts to smell, over and over again they pick the shirts of the men they would have healthier children with, according to their DNA samples. That's how powerful scent is. The article also said men are much more drawn to women when they are ovulating. They can tell by the pheromones that are emitted. (Remember that for your calendar when you are planning that next date, ladies.)

Another article said a queen bee's pheromones are so strong that she renders her faithful worker bees infertile and easier to control. (Don't remember that the next time you are planning your next date, ladies. That's just mean.) Queens also excrete especially strong pheromones when bees from the hive get lost. Her scent attracts the lost bees so much that they find their way home. (I also discovered that after these bees come home and the queen bee mates with them, they die immediately or are left out in the cold to freeze to death in the next season. Maybe bees are not the best role models for dating after all.)

Lesson learned: Pheromones are powerful, and mine were not displaying their feminine prowess like they should be. How could my sweet little awkward pheromones get the makeover my brother suggested? I came up with a plan of action.

The first strategy was to take loads of zinc. I read zinc is supposed to help your pheromones work better. I bought a big bottle at Vitamin Cottage and decided I would take three times the daily recommended dosage because, of course, then I would get three times as many dates.

My second strategy was to buy some pheromone perfume. I asked a friend what she thought about the idea, and she said, "Kate! You can't walk around with someone else's pheromones! What if a girl named Sylvia donated her pheromones to your perfume? And what if Joe, the guy you meet because of your pheromone perfume, is a creepy dude with gelled hair and a leather jacket with too many zippers? And what if Joe was really meant for Sylvia, and he was just drawn to you because you were wearing her pheromones?"

I could see her point. I decided to be safe and try out the plan for only a month to see what happened. The plan was simply taking a bunch of zinc every night and slathering some pheromone perfume on every morning.

Here is what happened:

1. Three girls at the middle school where I subbed asked me where I bought my perfume.

2. A guy with exactly nine zippers on his leather jacket asked me if I wanted to go to a wrestling match with him.

3. Four homeless men asked me to marry them.

4. I was stung by three bees.

Actually, none of that happened. Well, one homeless guy did ask me to marry him, but that occurs fairly often in my life.

What really happened is that I went on a trip to see a male friend of mine whom I had secretly liked for a long time, and I spilled every drop of my pheromone perfume onto every piece of clothing in my suitcase. I did not do that on purpose, but I wondered if God had *let* that pheromone perfume spill so this guy would be wildly attracted to me.

The trip went great. But nothing romantic happened between us, and he is now married to someone else. After that trip, I thought, *Maybe I can't fix my pheromones. Maybe there is something I can work on.*

At that point in my life, I had not tested the dating pool that much. I had been through a few long-term relationships and had gone on a few online dates that never worked out. It was time to get back out there.

So I spent the money I had used for that pricey pheromone perfume on a different strategy: online dating. Match, eHarmony, OkCupid, Christian Mingle, OnDaySix (because that's when God created man and woman, y'all)…you name it. If it had lots of profiles of men who said they loved camping, I was on it. I received a huge number of messages that ranged from "You glow in your profile picture" (which I did, because those were professional pictures taken in good lighting for my book) to "I have already married and divorced you in my mind."

I went on one of my first dates with a man I will call Rob. I was living in San Diego at the time, so we got lunch by the beach.

After some small talk (one of my least favorite things on the planet), he said to me, "All right, let's cut to the chase. If we don't have the same theology, this is not going to work. So: Do you believe in one God, the Father Almighty, Creator of heaven and earth?"

"Yes."

"Do you believe in Jesus Christ, his only Son, who was conceived by the virgin Mary and became a man?"

"Yes."

"The communion of saints? The forgiveness of sins? The resurrection of the dead?"

"Yes, yes, and yes."

Suddenly, my Catholic upbringing jogged my brain. "Are you rolling through the Apostle's Creed?"

"Well, at least you get points for knowing what that was."

As the conversation progressed, I talked about the ministry I did with hippies. He seemed wary of this and kept asking questions about it. I knew he was trying to weed out whether I was Unitarian.

He said to me, "So why are you not married? Are all the guys in your life blind?" (Three points for such a sweet question, Rob.) "I don't know. I guess it just hasn't been in the cards for me."

He replied, "What, like the *tarot cards*?" (The three points from the sweet question were now canceled out with that utterly judgmental question, making exactly zero points.)

"No. That's a common expression. *In the cards*."

"What, like the cards you use to *gamble with*?" (Now we are down to negative two, my friend.)

"Let's just say it hasn't happened for me yet."

Needless to say, that date ended, and we never saw each other again.

A few weeks later, I got a message from a man saying, "I don't live in San Diego, but I am here on business and would really like to meet you today. Do you have time?" He had an unusual name that rang a bell in my head, but I couldn't quite place it. "Well, why not?" I responded.

We texted each other to get to the place we were going. When we met, he was quite handsome and charming. He explained to me that he worked for a company that sold diet shake drinks through multilevel marketing. He was obviously passionate about his job. He touched my leg and said, "That's not why I have you here right now, of course. I just wanted to tell you about what I did."

Somewhere along the line, he said to me, "I noticed you have a 303 area code. That's Colorado. I live in Colorado."

"Where do you live?" I asked.

"In Boulder."

"I lived in Boulder for ten years!"

He said, "Wait a second. Are you the Kate who used to lead worship at Origins Church?"

"Yes!"

"I remember you!"

A guy from my small church in Boulder being matched with me on a dating website in San Diego? Maybe it was meant to be.

I took him to the airport at the end of our date (something I wouldn't normally do, but I felt I knew him because he used to go to Origins), and he left saying, "Well, now I have a good reason to come back to San Diego."

After I left he texted me saying, "I really enjoyed meeting you today. If you joined my team, we could stay really connected to each other." As in his multilevel marketing team. I told him I really enjoyed meeting him as well and that I would think about it.

Soon after, I talked to my mom and told her the story. She mentioned that she might be interested in what he did as she was looking for some work to do online.

A few weeks later, he texted me to tell me that he was coming back through San Diego. I got excited. *Maybe this will be what I have been waiting for!* I thought to myself.

He came to my house, and we decided to drive together downtown and then walk to the restaurant he had in mind. As we were walking downtown, a train was stuck on its tracks, and we couldn't get past it for about fifteen minutes. "This is so stupid," he kept saying. "I can't believe this." He was obviously easily frustrated. I started realizing this might not be the best date ever.

I mentioned to him that my mother might be interested in joining his team. "No, Kate," he said. "She is not the one who should be considering this. You should!"

"I love my job so much, and I'm not good at sales. This is not something I would like to be doing."

He replied, "You will have *more* time to do what you love! You will love the work. It's such a good product."

After I told him again that I wasn't interested, he kept pressing me. I said, "Can we talk about something else, please?"

We finally got past the train, but when we arrived at the restaurant he had wanted to go to, it was closed. He was more than just not happy about this—he was angry. Usually on the second date, you are still trying to put your best foot forward. But he didn't seem to mind showing me his frustration.

We kept walking, looking for a place to eat. I was super hungry. He looked up every restaurant we passed on Yelp and rejected each one, saying, "This doesn't have enough stars. We can't go here." I tried to tell myself he was simply trying to create a nice experience for me, but my hunger started to overwhelm those gestures.

We finally passed a simple hamburger place. "Look," I said, "I am so hungry, and I am hypoglycemic. I really need to eat something."

"Fine," he said angrily.

As we ate our two-and-a-half-star burgers, much to his chagrin, we made small talk. I told him at some point that I had Lyme disease and have had a lifelong struggle with insomnia. I also mentioned to him that I had struggled with depression in my life at times, but that I was in a good season now.

He said, "I know what can cure your insomnia! The shakes I sell! Or else marijuana."

I was surprised—but he wasn't finished.

"*And*," he said "I know exactly what can help you with your depression. I used to have anxiety really bad and I tried it once, and it completely cured me."

"What's that?" I asked, intrigued.

"Crystal meth."

This time I was shocked. "I'm sorry to have to break this to you, but I am never, *ever*, going to try crystal meth."

At this point he started yelling at me right in the middle of the restaurant, loudly enough that many of the people around us were staring. "You say you don't want to join my company, but you know nothing about it! It will change your life! And you tell me you are depressed and that you have insomnia, but you won't try any of my suggestions! I'm the only person in your life brave enough to tell you how messed up you are!"

Oh, wow. This was getting crazy. He said, "I'm just going to walk back to my car." It was a far walk, but I agreed that it was the best idea. We weren't going to be on eHarmony's front page as a success story after all.

And still, I did not give up. I went on date after date after date. Dozens of first dates, almost zero second dates. (I will say that I met two of my best guy friends on Christian Mingle, so the effort wasn't completely wasted. One of them almost choked on a piece of steak on our second date until I patted his back vigorously. Perhaps all of this was so he wouldn't die?)

Amid all the online dating, I was invited to a new adventure— speed dating.

I know, I know. The only thing lower on the dating totem pole than online dating is speed dating. But you have to take risks every once in a while, right?

Speed dating was like an auction. The bachelor walked across the stage and the caller said quickly and with a singsong voice, "Look at this lovely specimen of a man with the argyle socks and nice jawline. Can I get one date one date one date? Come on, ladies, how about a nice dinner and a movie? I see your one. One date one date can I get two dates? Come on, you lonely ladies, wouldn't you love for this handsome young man to take you bowling? I see you, lady in the fur coat, make that two dates two dates."

Okay, it was nothing like that, but it felt almost that frantic.

The party started out with mingling, which was especially awkward because we knew we were all there for the same reason—to get ourselves a few slow dates after these fast ones.

Next, all the girls were asked to sit in a chair. The hosts explained that a man would sit in the seat next to us, we would get five minutes to talk, and then a gong would ring. Then the men would move clockwise to the next seat.

This is when I started realizing something. I *hate* first dates. All the small talk makes me more nervous than a man with a combover in a wind tunnel. Now I was going to go through twelve awkward first dates in the space of an hour. What had I gotten myself into? This was either going to be a whole lot of fun or a whole lot of horrible. But like the time I went cliff jumping in college even though it was really dangerous, I knew I had to stop thinking about it. I just had to jump.

Here is a loosely translated rendition of what happened.

Gong. Enter sweet, short man with glasses who is balding a little bit.

"Hi, my name's Ed!"

"Hi, Ed!"

"I hate these things."

"I hate them too."

"Why are we even here?"

"Well, they said there would be good hummus."

Chuckle, chuckle.

"Have you ever tried online dating? That's even harder."

"Yes, I hated online dating. There wasn't even good cyber hummus."

Gong. Enter tall guy who is geeky but in kind of a cute way.

"Hi, I'm Walter. So you live in Golden Hill? Do you ever go to that great little ice-cream shop on Twenty-Fifth?"

"Yes, I love that ice-cream shop! In fact, my friends and I have this fun thing we do where we dress up like pirates and ride around on our bikes and end up there and eat ice cream with our eye patches on."

"Do you like reenacting characters?"

"Kind of. Just when we dress up and ride our bikes."

"Fascinating. I am really into Civil War reenactments."

"Do you travel to the South to do that?"

"No, I do it here in California."

"Was California even a state during the Civil War?"

"You obviously don't know much history."

"Well, in truth, Walter, I'm a pacifist. I don't like war when it really happens, let alone pretending to make it happen again later."

Gong. Enter my friend Brian. We laugh louder than we should because we are both so happy to see someone we know, and we want people to be impressed with how much fun we're having.

"So it looks like you decided to go as low on the dating totem pole as you possibly could."

"Well, looks like you did the same thing."

Gong. Enter hippie-looking guy named Ben.

"Are you a vegetarian? Because I'm a vegetarian."

"No, I'm hypoglycemic, so I eat copious amounts of meat every day. Also, I used to live on a meat farm."

"Murderer."

Silence.

"I mean…just kidding."

Gong. Enter cute hipster boy named Roy.

"I have an idea. Let's promise to not ask each other predictable questions. Ready, go!"

Silence. "I can't think of anything that's not predictable."

"What do you like on your pizza?

"Do you really think that will help us know if we should go on a real date?"

"I'm only going to date you if you like anchovies."

Chuckle, chuckle.

"What's your take on predestination?"

Silence.

"So, what do you like on your pizza?"

Gong. Enter guy I had been on a few dates with months ago. We'd become friends and talked occasionally. I'd had a crush on him from the start and had written to him about it a week before, but he hadn't responded. I was super surprised to see him there.

"I'm so sorry I didn't answer that last note from you. I have no excuse."

"That's okay. Really it's okay."

Silence.

I got through it. I did get one date out of the whole experience, which was flattering because so many pretty girls were there. It made me feel special. However, the guy was much younger. During the date, when he said, "I think I'm becoming a grown-up. As of last week, I don't eat cereal for every meal," I knew we might be in trouble.

I went through several more years of online dating. At times I would become really involved with it, and at times I would back away and not go on any dates for months. I also went on a few more unsuccessful speed dating nights, including one with four men and fourteen women. The experience left me disheartened.

But now, fast-forward to my present life. I wrote the first edition of this book a few years ago and was asked to write a few new chapters for the second edition, which included the chapter you are reading now. In the time between, I have miraculously met a man whom I have been dating for more than a year now. It seems as though he may even turn out to be the love of my life. He is perhaps the kindest, most loving human I know. He is a wonderful dad and one of the most vibrant Christians I have ever met. I didn't find him online or speed dating—he simply goes to the home group I attend. He is attracted to me even though I have gained weight the last few years and even though I threw away my pheromone perfume long ago.

He loves me more deeply than anyone ever has. He tells me every single day that I am beautiful, that I'm amazing, and that he loves me. As my boyfriend often tells me, "I was already happy because of God's love; you just make me happi*er*. You are my *er*." I have seen that, just as everyone told me, being in romantic relationship brings new joys and new sorrows, just like I had different joys and sorrows being single. But I must admit that it feels good to feel loved like this.

Yet even in the midst of being cared for in this way, I remind myself that my value doesn't come from what he thinks of me but what God thinks of me. His love for me can change sometimes, while God's love for me will never change. God's love is what sustains me. God has been there every moment of my life, and no one else can ever have that kind of place in my life.

Being with someone who loves me deeply like this has taught me a few lessons. I now know that my being single was not because I was undesirable or because I was not putting myself out there enough or not because my pheromones were lacking. It simply was not time yet. God was waiting for just the right season to bring us together, and we had a lot we had to work through to get to each other. No, I had not finally let go so God could bring *the one*. In fact, because of a previous breakup, when we met I was more broken about my singleness than I had ever been before. But sometimes God brings hope in the most unexpected places.

Does the fact that he is in my life negate this whole book for you? I hope not. I went through more than four decades alone before I got to this point. Whether or not this man will be my husband is something I continue praying about. I am trying to give it time.

The other day I was looking through some dusty old journals. I ran across some entries I'd written about a decade ago during a two-year relationship with a man who did not know the *entire time* whether he loved me or not. This drained the life out of my soul in small, painful seeps that entire length of time. As I read through those journal entries, I realized how hard I was on myself. I would get so mad at myself in that season for being too emotional. Too needy. Now that I'm with someone who knows he loves me, I realize I was not being too needy in that past relationship. My needs were just not getting met.

I read other entries where I was mad at myself for putting out a sister vibe with men I was interested in. I would also beat myself up for not knowing how to flirt. Now that I am with a man who is not afraid of commitment, I realize that oftentimes it was not my fault these men were treating me like a sister—they were just not the most committed of men. I wasn't broken. My picker was broken.

I realized that I, the girl reading these journals, had become older but also had become more content in her own skin and was kinder to herself. I started wondering: What would squishy, happier, older me say to younger, more toned, more frantic me?

She would say, *Don't worry. You're doing the best you can. This is all scary and hard. Give yourself grace.*

She would say, *Buy that pheromone perfume if it makes you feel better. You can try to lose some weight if that's what you think is best and it doesn't take over your life. But God sees your beauty even if your pheromones are malfunctioning, and he thinks you are amazing no matter what you look like. If you are looking for a mate, it would be good to look for someone who will do the same.*

She would say, *I know it's hard sometimes, but trust God. The longer I live, the more I see that he is more trustworthy than you can imagine.*

What about you? What would current, squishy, kind you say to younger, fit, anxious you? And what if you could reach forward and ask future really squishy, really old, really wise you to talk to the beautiful girl who sits reading this chapter right now? What would she say to you? What advice would she give? Can you hear her kind voice now?

Maybe she would give us less advice about our outer world (Wear pheromone perfume! Date online! Try harder!) and more about our inner world (Believe you are beautiful. There is nothing you can do for God to love you any more or any less. It's time to trust. Be kind to yourself. Do the next right thing.).

Let your older, squishy self, the one who wears rosewater instead of someone else's pheromones, grab hands with the Holy Spirit, and let their two hands lead you down this path. With all of this wisdom between us, we will surely find our way.

The Deepest Love Story

> Nothing is more practical…than falling in love in an absolute, final way. What you are in love with, what seizes your imagination, will affect everything. It will decide what will get you out of bed in the morning, what you will do with your energy, how you spend your weekends, what you read, who you know, what breaks your heart, and what amazes you with joy and gratitude. Fall in love, stay in love, and it will decide everything.
>
> Pedro Arrupe

A few years ago, a dear friend of mine took a class on myths. In it, he learned stories from different cultures and religions around the world and saw so many common threads that he began to doubt whether any of them were true. He wondered if the story he grew up with—the story of Jesus—was just another myth.

My friend came away from that class pretty sure that none of the stories, not even the Jesus stories, really happened.

I have thought a lot about his experience, and what I have concluded is that the similarities between myths do not suggest that none of the stories are true, but instead that there is one root story. The Great Love Story from which all other stories flow.

The deepest, most beautiful love story.

I don't think there could possibly be a deeper story than the one I believe in. Since this book is about love, I want to explore this mysterious story. Though you might have heard it many times, I want you to try to hear it as if you were hearing it for the first time.

It goes like this:

Once upon a time, there was a God who was so blindingly beautiful that when he spoke, stars would come forth. When he walked, life would spring up everywhere. When he breathed, love would pour out of him like water. He did not simply have hope and love and passion living within him; he was hope and love and passion. He was light, and darkness could not live in the light.

He was love and love must be shared, so he breathed into dirt and his image became a man. From the beginning of that man's life, God wanted to give him the greatest gift: the gift of intimacy, of oneness. So he gave Adam himself, and he also gave Adam a counterpart, a companion.

The counterpart was called woman, and the two were made as one.

From the very beginning, God did not want slaves; he wanted a family. He gave the two a choice: They could turn their backs on him, or they could run toward him. Their power to choose reflected that they were made in God's image. God set before them death and life, blessings and curses, the knowledge of good and the knowledge of evil.

They chose to turn against him.

Because darkness cannot live in the light, God was separated from his beloved, and his heart was broken.

We who have had our hearts broken may think we are the only ones who have faced the pain of unrequited love, but our God has suffered through it like no one else ever has. Sometimes, when I struggle with rejection, I ask God, "Have you ever gone through this?"

God's answer? "Every day."

In *The Divine Romance,* Gene Edwards explores the unrequited love God had for his people in the Old Testament.

> He had stood there all morning…watching intently toward the south. Finally, in the late afternoon, it began

to appear, first as a tiny speck on the horizon, gradually growing until it became a moving sea of humanity. It was his people, lately set free from slavery…He stared at this moving mass of humanity until the image before him blurred and began to change in form and, finally, became one person. His eyes now saw not a multitude of people, but only a lovely young girl, coming up from Egypt, crossing the hot sands and moving toward him…Again and again he issued forth to her a cry: Return to me. Return to me![1]

Many stories in the Old Testament give imagery to God's broken heart toward this girl. One of the most poignant is the story of Hosea.

God asks his prophet Hosea to marry a prostitute named Gomer. Hosea does so, and Gomer ends up having affairs with other men and prostituting herself even while she is married to him. The book's language is often disturbing, full of pain, frustration, and anger. However, behind all of it is God's deep, groaning desire for his loved one to come back. He longs for his counterpart—his beloved—to return to him.

As a foreshadowing of what was to come, God says to Hosea, "Go, show your love to your wife again, though she is loved by another and is an adulteress. Love her as the LORD loves the Israelites, though they turn to other gods…So [Hosea] bought her for fifteen shekels of silver" (Hosea 3:1-2).

Did you catch that? He bought his wife back.

Imagine what Gomer the prostitute went through when her husband bought her back. She chose to sell herself to men who abused her and destroyed her self-worth rather than to stay with a good man who loved her deeply and tenderly.

Can you picture the scene? She is standing in the local square, peddling herself to the highest bidder. She is dirty and bloody from the men who have beaten her and treated her like their property.

Hosea steps in front of her. She sees him and is ashamed. This is the only man who has ever truly loved her. The only man who has given himself to her instead of taking from her. The only man who has seen her for who she is and still loves her, even in her brokenness. But she has left him. She has forsaken him. How would he ever want her back?

In this scene, she is wearing the garments of a harlot, and she is exposed. Hosea sees Gomer in all of her sin. Is he going to make a public spectacle of her like she deserves? Is he going to beat her for leaving him? Will he stone her for her unfaithfulness, which would be completely acceptable in that day?

He does none of these things. Even though he is her husband and has rights over her, he shows her how deeply he loves her. He shows her she is valuable to him. Astonishingly, Hosea walks up to the man who currently owns his wife and hands him his money. He picks his wife up into his loving arms, kisses her, and carries her home.

These are the loving words that God speaks to his beloved:

> Therefore I am now going to allure her; I will lead her into the desert and speak tenderly to her. There I will give her back her vineyards, and I will make the Valley of Achor* into a doorway of hope. There she will sing as in the days of her youth, as in the days she came up out of Egypt. In that day…you will call me "my husband." You will no longer call me "my master." I will betroth you to me forever; I will betroth you in righteousness and justice, in love and compassion. I will betroth you in faithfulness, and you will acknowledge† the Lord…I will show my love to the one called "Not my loved one." I will say to those called "Not my people," "You are my people"; and they will say, "You are my God" (Hosea 2:14-16,18,19-20,23).

---

* "trouble"

† or, "intimately know"

In that day he will change our name from "abandoned" to "loved," from "orphan" to "the one with a home."

The story of Hosea wasn't just a love story between one man and a prostitute. It was the story of one God and a world that had turned against him, a world that he longed to know intimately again.

After centuries of God's wooing and his beloved rejecting, the day finally came for the mystery of the world to be revealed. The day that he would reconcile his beloved back to himself.

The God of the universe, the God who contains eternity, made himself small. So small, in fact, that we could hold him in our arms, close to our hearts. He was a child named Emmanuel, which means "God with us." This incarnation is, in itself, a mystery beyond understanding.

That child grew up to be a man. He fought for the rights for the poor, the rights for the outcast. It seemed that the more people hated these sinners, the more Jesus loved them, much like Hosea loved the prostitute so many years before. Jesus spoke identity and worth into those the world deemed worthless. He saw them like no one else had seen them; he loved them like no one had loved them.

As I wrote in my song "Mary's Song,"

> You called out my name
> It's like I heard it for the first time.
> I was wretched and ashamed
> But you saw me like no one has seen me.
> You said, "You've had many lovers
> Who love themselves when you are near
> But I alone have known you
> And I love you like no one has loved you."
> I said, "I am broken I have nothing left to bring."
> You said, "Vessels must be broken to pour out an
>   offering."
> So I pour all my tears out and I bend to kiss the feet

Of the one who sees me lovely
The one who sees me beautiful.[2]

God's love for us and the new names he gave us came with a
price, though. To truly see us holy, to completely see us beautiful, he
knew that he had to eradicate the darkness and tear down the walls
between him and his people.

He knew that laws couldn't bring us back. We would never be
holy enough to approach him. The only answer was to pay our pun-
ishment for us, to buy us back like Hosea bought back his wife. And
so he gave up his life. The most precious commodity on earth, the
blood of God himself, was poured out to purchase us. That's how
valuable we are to him.

He hung on that cross like a "lamb slain from the foundation of
the world" (Revelation 13:8). He did not just hang on a hill called
Calvary; he hung above eternity, above time.

Henri Nouwen talks about his time at L'Arche, a home for men-
tally handicapped adults. One Good Friday, all of the handicapped
people and their workers gathered together. He and the other priests
took down the cross that hung behind the altar and held it so that
everyone could come touch it.

As he stood there with his beloved handicapped friends, Nouwen pictured Jesus with his arms open over a world filled with great
suffering:

> Imagining the naked, lacerated body of Christ stretched
> out over our globe, I was filled with horror. But as I
> opened my eyes I saw Jacques, who bears the marks of
> suffering in his face, kiss the body with passion and tears
> in his eyes. I saw Ivan carried on Michael's back. I saw
> Edith coming in her wheelchair. As they came—walk-
> ing or limping, seeing or blind, hearing or deaf—I saw
> the endless procession of humanity gathering around
> the sacred body of Jesus, covering it with their tears and
> their kisses, and slowly moving away from it comforted

and consoled by such great love…With my mind's eye I saw the huge crowds of isolated, agonizing individuals walking away from the cross together. Bound by the love they had seen with their own eyes and touched with their own lips. The cross of horror became the cross of hope, the tortured body became the body that gives new life; the gaping wounds became the source of forgiveness, healing, and reconciliation.[3]

This is what Jesus did for us on the cross that hung above the world. He met us in our suffering.

As Jesus hung suspended over time, war, disease, pain, divorce, poverty, and hell itself were driven into him, and they were immersed in his all-encompassing love. The angels flew to the end of history; they captured suffering and sin and threw it on him. This happened beyond time. That is why we have victory over darkness even now while we suffer on the earth.

The final thing that Jesus took upon his tortured body was death itself.

And then, the veil of the temple was ripped in two. It was no longer just the high priest who could approach God face-to-face once a year. Now, all people had access to him. We see a representation of this beautiful picture when two people are married and the bride wears a veil. The moment after the covenant is announced, the two are asked to kiss. The veil is lifted. In essence, the bride says, "Up to this point, I have not made myself completely vulnerable to you. You have known part of me, but you have not known all of me. I lift this veil because now is the time for love. I am making myself completely vulnerable to you. Vulnerability means risk and pain, but ultimately, it means intimacy."

When Jesus spread his arms open on that cross, he made himself completely vulnerable. The veil was torn in two, lifted, so we could see the face of God. He lifts up the veil and he sees us, as well, made beautiful for the first time because of his sacrifice. Every part of us is brought into the open. Instead of being rejected we are kissed. We are fully accepted. We are fully loved.

But this is still not the end of the Greatest Love Story.

One day, one glorious day, a wedding will take place. The bride that God fought for throughout all history—the one he gave his life for—will finally come.

Again from *The Divine Romance*:

> A door opens in the new heavens…the New Jerusalem. A city of a hundred million shining stones, each glowing with the glory of the light that is its center. And the center is the Lord, Christ Jesus!
>
> The city begins its descent, and, as it does, it begins to change. A galaxy of living light is swirling downward in the skies. Gradually the stardust of light becomes a multitude of people—the vast host of the redeemed, the multitude no man can number.
>
> The brightness grows, the lights become all one. At the center of this light, a form begins to emerge.
>
> Standing before them is the Bride of the Lamb.
>
> Her eyes have never seen or known one glimpse of the tragedies that befell her in the old creation. She stands there in the strength and perfection of youth. Her glowing visage tells a thousand tales of love, of passion, of singular devotion to her Lord.
>
> The woman begins to glow with a brightness far beyond the ends of belief. The glory of the brightness of the Lord ignites with a fire that immerses, and then consumes all else.
>
> Forever! No more alone.[4]

This is the deepest love story. The story from which all other stories flow. Whether we know it or not, this is the story we live in.

In the end, it will not really matter if you are single or married or divorced, if you are beautiful or ugly, if you are abandoned or cherished.

You are the Beloved. Forever, no more alone.

Afterword

You are stronger than you think you are.

You, your hands dirtied with the soil where you till up the rocks of generations gone by. Your tears watering the ground, making the roots grow deep and wide while you are unaware. You labor, you dig, you claw this tiny piece of land where others buried their dreams and gave up trying.

But not you. You keep going. You never give up. You see the tree in the seed, and you will fight until that tree is standing before you, its long, willowing arms grasping your hope in its branches.

You are stronger than you think you are.

You, covered in all your scars. Where your face was grazed with false imaginings that you were not beautiful enough. Where your hands were caught in fields of cotton when you didn't believe you were free. Where you were marked across your chest the day you thought that they left because you weren't worth it. Look closely, love. Look closely because those scars are gilded with gold. Those scars have become your crown.

You are stronger than you think you are.

You, dancing there with your face against the wind. Not a pretty dance, but a wild dance. A hold-on-for-dear-life-to-the-hope dance. An I-will-never-stop-believing-in-your-goodness dance. A shake-the-sadness-off-your-skin dance. You, with your feet pounding against the ground to the rhythm of your unsurrendering spirit. With your knees soiled and bleeding from the prayers and the longings and the times you almost gave up. With your arms thrown up in surrender and beckoning and awe. "You are my love!" you yell, "And I will never stop believing!" There is burning against your back as you lift up your face, because your wings are returning, love. Your wings are returning.

Look at me and believe now. You are stronger than you think you are. Stronger than you think you are.

Group Study Guide

By Kate Hurley with Calley Crews

If you would like Kate and Calley, a licensed professional counselor and addiction counselor, to lead a weekend or day retreat with your group, you can contact Kate through her website, katehurley.com.

Here are a few guidelines for your group:

1. **Create a safe environment.** There should be a code of confidentiality within this group. Nothing shared should go beyond these four walls. Try hard not to judge each other so that everyone will feel safe to share. Remember that everyone's journey is valid and beautiful.

2. **Listen, listen, listen.** Avoid cross talk. Let people finish their thoughts. Avoid pat answers or too much advice giving. Try asking more questions instead of coming up with more answers. Make sure that the quieter members get heard as much as the more talkative members.

3. **Challenge yourself and others to be honest and open.** Henri Nouwen said, "What is most personal is also the most universal." Often when we open up it allows others to know that they are not alone.

4. **Try hard to read the chapters assigned to each week.** It will be difficult to participate if the material isn't read. If reading is not something you are used to, try to read

for fifteen minutes a night before bed. That should be
enough time to cover the chapters.

5. **Journal.** Bring a journal and pen to this group, as there
will be a lot of writing. Leaders might want to have
some paper and pens on hand in case someone forgets.

6. **Be mindful of the time.** Leaders, make sure to keep your
eye on this. Oftentimes there are hands-on activities
during the lessons. Look for these before you start the
meeting so you get an idea of where they are in the
lesson and how long they might take. These are an
important part of the meeting, as they allow people to
own what they are learning. Make sure to leave enough
time for these. (They will usually take at least half an
hour to do and discuss.)

7. **Have one-on-one time.** Meet with members of your
group one on one. Leaders, challenge yourselves to do
this. It really bonds the group. Keep a special eye out
for people who might feel left out and consider making
time to help them feel loved and accepted.

Week 1:
Getting to Know You

Before the first meeting, everyone should read the Introduction
and first two chapters.

1. Start out by going over the guidelines on pages 233-34.

2. Time each person for ten to twenty minutes. (Change
the time according to how many people you have in

your group.) Share with the group a timeline of your life—your personal story. Share as much as you are comfortable with. Some things you can highlight are your heritage, high points, low points, and how God worked throughout it.

3. If you have time left before the timer goes off, ask the person questions about their life or comment on how you see God's work in their life.

Homework: Read chapters 3 and 4.

Next week will be a pity party! It will be a time when we can talk honestly about some of our struggles as singles. Bring pity party food, and if you want to you can dress in pajamas and bring your favorite break-up song.

Week 2:
Pity Party

Today we are going to focus on healing from wounds having to do with romantic relationships.

1. Share some of your worst dating and break-up stories.

2. Chapter 3 talks about letting ourselves be honest with the way that we feel about our singleness. Go around the room and let yourselves "rant." What has been difficult about being single? Have you been honest about these struggles or have you stuffed them inside of you?

3. This chapter talks about disenfranchised loss, a loss that stems from not having something that you desire. Talk about this idea. What kind of disenfranchised losses

have you had? Why do you think the loss associated with singleness is often overlooked in the church?

4. In this chapter we explored the story of Hannah, who was honest with God about her frustration and pain. How does her story inspire you? Have you felt like you can talk to God with this much honesty? Why or why not?

5. Chapter 4 talks about the stories that we have been surrounded with, from books we read as children to movies we watched as adults. These stories immerse us in the idea that romantic love is the key to a happy ending. What do you think about this idea? How has the media affected you as a single person?

6. Go to a quiet place and write a letter to God about your walk through dating, break-ups, and singleness. Be honest by pouring out your heart to him, even if it sounds sad or angry at times.

7. Come back together and pray for each other about these issues.

Homework: Read chapters 5, 6, and 7.

Week 3:
Expectations and Gratitude

1. Chapter 5 says, "This is what happens when you are consumed by unmet expectations. If you're not careful, your expectations will steal away your joy." Can you think of a time in your life when your unmet expectations stole away your joy?

2. How do you think your expectations of what marriage will look like could put pressure on your potential future spouse?

3. Do you ever adhere to the idea that getting married will calm the deep aching that you might struggle with? Do you think this belief is really true? Where do you think that idea came from? How does church culture contribute to this?

4. In chapter 6, we talk about how each person is a bundle of strengths and weaknesses. How do you think your acceptance of your own weaknesses will help you accept other people, including your potential future spouse?

5. In chapter 7, we talk about recognizing the gifts that have been given us today. What is something in your life that you fervently prayed for in the past that has now been answered? Do you take it for granted now?

6. "He did not wait for the victory to be thankful. His thankfulness is what brought the victory." How can gratitude bring victory even before your prayers are answered? How can thankfulness defeat the enemy, as in the story of Jehoshaphat?

7. Go to a quiet place and write down five prayers that have been answered by God in your life. Thank him for these answered prayers. Now write down five prayers that haven't been answered. Ask God how you can be thankful even in the midst of these unanswered prayers.

Homework: Read chapter 8 and keep a log of things you are thankful for throughout the week. Try to notice them as they come and jot them down as soon as possible. Challenge yourself to write down five a day, or even more.

Week 4:

Changing Your Name

Make sure to leave enough time for the exercise at the end of this lesson. It will take at least 45 minutes if you include sharing and prayer time.

1. In chapter 8 we learn about Jacob, whose name meant "supplanter." This could be defined as one who wants to be what he is not. Have you ever wished that you had someone else's job, someone else's looks, someone else's relationship status, someone else's children, someone else's life? Why do you think comparison is a problem we face as human beings?

2. As Jacob strove to be the firstborn, something he could never be, he became a control freak. Do you ever find yourself striving to control things that may be out of your control? Where do you think this desire comes from?

3. Do you think there is anything in life that you can control besides your own reaction to things? Do you ever try to control by ruminating about things or even by praying "hard enough"?

4. Take time to write down some negative names and/ or ungodly beliefs that you have about yourself. Get together with a partner to talk about that belief. Then work together to write the opposite. Some examples:

Ungodly Beliefs
I don't belong. I am always left out.
I am a failure.

I will always be lonely.

If you see the real me, you will reject me.

My value is only in what I do.

If I don't plan and control things, my life will fall apart.

I am unattractive.

I will always be_____ (insecure, jealous, fearful).

Godly Beliefs

I do belong. People like being around me.

I am not a failure.

Even if I am lonely, God will comfort me and will give
me seasons of family.

People who see the real me will love me, because I am
lovable.

My value is not in what I do but in who I am.

I do not have to control things. God holds my life in
his hands.

I am beautiful.

I will always be _____ (loved, precious, a
daughter of God).

Now, go to a quiet place and write a letter from Jesus to you. Ask him to tell you how he has replaced your old names with new ones. Try to listen and hear him talk about the way that he sees you. Come back together and share these if there is time.

Homework: Read chapters 9 and 10. Try to notice the lies that are running through your head. Make a conscious decision to replace the lies with truth. If you want, you can invite a married friend or friends next week to have a dialogue about what married and single people can learn from one another.

Week 5:
What Singles Wish Married People Knew...and Vice Versa

Write down three formulas or hurtful things that well-meaning friends (or church culture) have said to you in regards to your singleness.

1. Share your three formulas. Why do you think people say things like this? (Remember that most of the time they don't have ill intentions.)

2. Have you ever felt that your singleness is a result of your doing something wrong? Where do you think this idea came from?

3. What are some lessons you can learn (both good and bad) from your own parents' marriage? Other friends' marriages?

4. Read the section on the removal of the projections out loud. The advice given is, "Wait to get engaged until the removal of the projections happens." Can you see the wisdom in waiting for this process to happen while you are dating rather than after you get married? Do you have examples of past relationships where the removal of the projections happened and you were surprised at what you saw in the other person after some time had passed? Why do you think taking things slowly with someone you are dating is a good idea?

5. Is communicating scary for you? How did your family communicate? Do you think that affected the way you communicate now? What does it mean to let go of the outcome?

6. Was the idea of a person's "code book" new for you? How do you think learning someone's code book can help a relationship? Can you think of some things in your own code book? Other people you know? How can you communicate your code book to other people in order to enrich the relationship?

7. Page 125 talks about the word *helpmate*. Did this definition surprise you? How so? How can being opposite of each other be a help rather than a hindrance?

Homework: Read chapters 11 and 12. Try to seek out a married friend this week. Ask them something they have learned in their years being married. Take it to heart and think about it. If you'd like, write it down to share with the group next week.

Week 6:
Navigating Dating

1. Did you ever write a list of qualities you wanted in a future mate (or did you keep a running list in your mind)? What was on the list? Which of these things were really important, and which were not that important? What are some of the plusses and minuses of having a list like this?

2. What is your philosophy on dating? Do you think it's okay to date casually? What are your thoughts on sex before marriage? Hopefully you feel safe enough to share your experiences with this, no matter what your journey has been in this area.

3. Do you think there is danger in relying too much on

signs from God when it comes to whom you will marry? Why or why not?

4. Do you want to know if you want to marry someone within the first few dates? Do you think this idea has put pressure on people, especially Christian men, when it comes to dating?

5. Write a "new list" for qualities you desire in a spouse. Think about the non-negotiables. Narrow the list down to only three or four things.

6. Often, we focus on a list for our future mate without looking at the kind of mate we would be for our spouse. People usually attract someone who is as healthy—or as unhealthy—as they are themselves. It would be wise to challenge ourselves to be the right person instead of just trying to find the right person. Write down qualities of the kind of spouse/person you want to be and steps you can take toward achieving that goal. (If you want to be respectful toward your mate, make a commitment to be careful with the way you talk about your friends now. If you want to be emotionally healthy, make a commitment to go to counseling even while you are single. If you want to be a good communicator, commit to reading books about communicating.) Know that even if you don't get married, bringing these gifts to the world will make it a better place. Come together and share your lists with each other.

Homework: Read chapters 13 and 14.

Week 7:
The Prodigal Son

1. Chapter 13 tells the story of a dear friend of Kate's who almost died. Have you ever had a situation in your life that made you realize how precious life is? Do you still think about the lessons you learned on a day-to-day basis, or did they fade as time went on?

2. Chapter 14 tells the story of the younger and older sons in the Prodigal Son story. Which brother do you relate to more? Why?

3. The younger son essentially says to his father, "I don't want your love; I want your loot." Have you ever said this to God?

4. The older son essentially says, "I have worked for you my whole life, and you have not rewarded me by giving me the desires of my heart." Have you ever said this to God?

5. If you are honest with yourself, do you struggle with the idea of God's goodness or even his existence because of the circumstances in your life?

6. Psalm 131:2 says, "I have calmed and quieted myself, I am like a weaned child with its mother; like a weaned child I am content." Do you think your prayer life often looks like going to God to get what you want like an infant, or more like a weaned child, where you go just to be with him? What steps could you take to move toward the latter?

7. Have someone read the Prodigal Son story in Luke 15:11-32 out loud. Read slowly, taking breaths intermittently to pause and think about the story. As

they are reading, close your eyes and picture yourself in the story. Put yourself in the shoes of the older or younger son, or even the father. At the end of the reading, leave space in your imagination to let the father run to you and talk to you about how he loves you as a child, not a slave. Let God speak to you for a while. If there is time, have someone read it again, perhaps putting yourself in the place of another character in the story. Journal what you heard and saw and talk to each other about the experience.

Homework: Read chapters 15, 16, and 17.

Week 8:
Building Your Own Family

1. Do you long to have a spouse and children? Talk about this longing. Has it been a dream since your childhood? How has waiting for this dream affected your relationship with God? If this longing were never filled, what would that be like for you?

2. Do you think society puts a stigma on people in their thirties and forties who still haven't gotten married or had children? Do big birthdays like twenty-five, thirty, or forty make you feel insecure? Why?

3. Chapter 15 talks about the importance of community in a single person's life. Do you remember a time when you were surrounded by people who were like family to you? What was that like? Do you remember another time

when you felt isolated? What do you think contributed to the isolation?

4. Do you think our society sacrifices connection for comfort sometimes? (Watching TV, Facebook, etc.) Do you think you do? Do you think the pursuit of happiness that was written into our Declaration of Independence is the highest goal we should have? If not, what is?

5. What steps can you take to keep community and connection sacred?

6. The book asks you to do an assignment that helps you understand God's heart for people who are in need. Let's try this assignment now. Take out your Bible and go to a quiet place for ten minutes. Without using a concordance, flip open your Bible and mark down every time you find that God talks about the poor, the outcast, the widow, the fatherless, the needy, the alien, or anything similar. Gather back together and read some of the verses to each other.

7. Were you surprised at how many of these verses you found? Did you know that there are some two thousand references to the poor in the Bible? What does this tell you about the heart of the Father?

8. Go to a quiet place again. Write down thoughts you have about building your own family. Write down a few practical ways that you can build community into your life or take care of people in need, both things that will give you a sense of belonging and purpose. Some examples are serving at a soup kitchen, starting a community garden, adopting a Compassion child, or starting a book club. Come back together and share these with your group. Try to ask each other about

these dreams in the weeks to come to keep each other
accountable.

*Homework: Read "How to Make Decisions" on page 50 and con-
template it during the week.*

Week 9:
What Would You Do
If You Weren't Afraid?

How to Make Decisions:

1. Figure out your truth. Not anyone else's. Yours.
2. Ask yourself, "What would I do if I weren't afraid?"
3. Do the next right thing.

1. Have one person read one of the steps above and then
   expound on what they think it means. Do that with
   each step.

2. Asking yourself what you would do if you weren't afraid
   can be used both for our overarching purpose in life
   and also for specific situations. What are some smaller
   situations in your life where you have fears? What would
   you do if you weren't afraid? What is the next right thing
   to do? Write these down and discuss.

3. Go to a quiet place. Pray and ask God for wisdom.
   Write down the answer to these questions in your
   journal:

4. Who do I love? (What kinds of people are you drawn to?
   Homeless? Children? At-risk youth? People who have

misunderstood God? Last week's discussion might have helped you with this.)

5. What makes me come alive?

6. What has God uniquely gifted me in?

7. What have I done that I am really proud of?

8. What do I wish I could do that I haven't done yet?

9. What are some fears I have when it comes to my purpose? What would I do if I weren't afraid? What is the next right thing to do in order to see these things happen in my life?

10. After writing these down, think about all of these answers and write a mission statement for your life. It should be concise, something you can remember. Work on it until it is just right. Kate's is a good example: To paint an accurate picture of a passionate God.

11. Come together and talk about what you wrote down. Pray for each other.

Homework: Read chapter 18 and the afterword.

Week 10:

Finding Your Place in the Deepest Love Story

Leaders: Bring candles for this session. Half as many candles as there are people should work.

1. Chapter 18 talks about the beautiful love story of God and his people. Have you ever thought about the

gospel as the deepest love story from which all of the other beautiful stories in the world flow? What favorite movies and/or stories have you read that are a reflection of the deepest love story? How is your life a reflection and part of the deepest love story?

2. Are there any parts of this story that were new to you or that you saw differently?

3. To end our study together, we are going to take some time to impart vision and destiny to each other. Take a candle to someone in the group. Go to a quiet place. Talk to that person about what you see in them…the gifts God has given them, the way they have shaped your life, the way you see them changing the world. Be quiet for a while and ask God for pictures or scriptures that might bless that person. Pray for them. Then have them do the same for you. If you have a recording device on your phone, you can record these so you can keep them. Take notes of anything that was said to you that you want to remember. Keep doing this until you have gotten to do the same thing with everyone in the group.

4. Come back together and discuss what you have learned in this study.

5. Read the afterword out loud. Remind each other that you are beautiful and strong. Speak out a prayer thanking God for seeing us as beautiful no matter what our circumstances may be.

Notes

Preface

1. This preface was inspired by the poem "Blue House" by Tomas Tonstörmer in *The Great Enigma: New Collected Poems*, trans. Robin Fulton (New York: New Directions Publishing Corporation, 2006).

Introduction

1. Eric Klinenberg, *Going Solo: The Extraordinary Rise and Surprising Appeal of Living Alone* (New York: Penguin Press, 2012).

Chapter 1

1. Linda Lyons, "What Frightens America's Youth?" Gallup.com, March 29, 2005, http://www.gallup.com/poll/15439/what-frightens-americas-youth.aspx.

2. David Blaine, interview by Guy Raz, *Ted Talk Radio Hour,* podcast audio, May 23, 2014, http://www.npr.org/programs/ted-radio-hour/312542881/what-we-fear.

Chapter 2

1. Kate Hurley, "Hey Little Girl," *Sleeping When You Woke Me*, 2007.

2. Kate Hurley, "You Are Not Alone," *Sleeping When You Woke Me*, 2007.

3. Kate Hurley, "Joy Comes in the Morning," *Weak and Strong at the Same Time*, 2010.

4. Alcoholics Anonymous, *The Big Book* (New York: Alcoholics Anonymous World Services, Inc., 2001).

5. Dr. Shauna Young in Durango, Colorado (assertivewellness.com), has cured people of Lyme disease, cancer, autism, and many other illnesses. If you are struggling with a chronic illness or seeking a diagnosis, it is worth consulting with her.

Chapter 3

1. Deborah Fileta, "Marriage Does Not Solve Your Problems," *Relevant*, May 23, 2012, http://www.relevantmagazine.com/life/relationship/features/29263-marriage -doesnt-solve-your-problems.

2. Melody Notkin, "My Secret Grief: Over 35, Single and Childless," Huffington Post,

January 12, 2002, http://www.huffingtonpost.com/melanie-notkin/my-secret-grief-over-35-s_b_1202808.html.

3. The section on Hannah was inspired by a teaching given by Ray Hughes. Learn more about Ray at selahministries.com.

4. Cheryl Strayed, *Tiny Beautiful Things* (New York: Vintage Books, 2012).

5. Kate Hurley, "Love of My Life," *Sing Over Me*, 2013.

6. Kate Hurley, "I Have Overcome," *Sing Over Me*, 2013.

Chapter 4

1. Ira Glass, *This American Life*, podcast audio, March 3, 2000, http://www.thisamericanlife.org/radio-archives/episode/153/dolls.

2. David Colman, "The Unsettling Stories of Two Lonely Dolls," *The New York Times*, October 17, 2004.

3. Dare Wright, *The Lonely Doll* (New York: Houghton Mifflin, 1957).

4. Vivian Paley, interview by Ira Glass, *This American Life*, podcast audio, March 3, 2000, http://www.thisamericanlife.org/radio-archives/episode/153/dolls.

5. Steven Pressfield, *The War of Art: Break Through the Blocks and Win Your Inner Creative Battles* (New York: First Black Irish Entertainment, 2002).

Chapter 5

1. Hara Estroff Marano, "The Expectation Trap," *Psychology Today*, March 1, 2010, http://www.psychologytoday.com/articles/201003/the-expectations-trap.

2. William Doherty, in Marano, "The Expectation Trap," *Psychology Today*, March 3, 2010.

3. Henri Nouwen, *The Wounded Healer* (New York: Doubleday, 1975).

Chapter 6

1. Graham Cooke, "The Inheritance-Jonathan David Helser (and Graham Cooke)," YouTube video, 8:33, posted by "Deni Huttula," August 17, 2007, http://www.youtube.com/watch?v=dEisSxR2cps.

2. Henri Nouwen, *Seeds of Hope: A Henri Nouwen Reader,* ed. Robert Durback (New York: Doubleday, 1997).

3. Thomas Merton, *No Man Is an Island* (New York: Houghton Mifflin Harcourt, 2002), 168.

Chapter 7

1. Meister Eckhart, quoted in J. John and Mark Stibbe, *A Bucket of Surprises* (London: Monarch, 2002).

Chapter 8

1. As quoted in John Hayes, *Sub-merge* (Ventura, CA: Regal Books, 2006).

2. A more in-depth account of this inspiring story can be found in the above-referenced book by John Hayes, *Sub-merge*.

3. Wes Bridel, "First-born: Birthright and Inheritance—Part 2," Kingdomcalling.com, June 20, 2009, http://www.kingdomcalling.com/2009/06/29/first-born-birthright -and-inheritance.

4. David Wilkerson, "Jabbok! A Place of Total Surrender," World Challenge Pulpit Series, accessed August 6, 2014, http://www.tscpulpitseries.org/english/undated/ tsjabbok.html.

5. C.S. Lewis, *A Grief Observed* (New York: HarperCollins, 1989).

Chapter 9

1. Donald Miller, *Searching for God Knows What* (Nashville: Thomas Nelson, 2010).

Chapter 10

1. Jad Abumrad and Robert Krulwich, *Radiolab*, podcast audio, August 28, 2007, http:// www.radiolab.org/story/91744-this-is-your-brain-on-love/.

2. Danny Silk, "Danny Silk, Covenant in Relationships," YouTube video, 1:22:55, from a teaching given at VerticalCall on December 4, 2011, posted by "ELIatVerticalCall," May 17, 2012, http://www.youtube.com/watch?v=Aj9rryTbbhc.

3. Dann Farrelly, *Brave Communication: Empowering Skills that Transform Relationships*, DVD.

4. This definition of *helpmate* is discussed in more detail by Bill Johnson in his teaching "Transformed People Transform Cities: Being a Bride" (disc 6).

Chapter 11

1. https://www.facebook.com/TheStorytellerStudios/posts/mr-rogers-carried-a-note -in-his-pocket-given-to-him-by-a-social-worker-the-note-/590908370971559/.

Chapter 12

1. Amy Dickinson, interview by Ira Glass, *This American Life*, podcast audio, February 10, 2006, http://www.thisamericanlife.org/radio-archives/episode/308/star-crossed-love.

2. This observation and others like it can be found on the website *Things About Love:* http://www.thingsaboutlove.com/what-does-love-mean.

Chapter 13

1. "Young, Free, and Amish," YouTube video, 4:09, posted by "National Geographic," October 26, 2010, http://www.youtube.com/watch?v=5lKlBPdgA_E.

2. I attended a group called the Single Life Workshop for a year, and it was a great model

for exactly this kind of singles group. Our small groups were co-ed and we talked about very deep issues like pornography and sexual abuse as well as things like being good communicators. Find out more about bringing groups like this to your own community at www.singlelifeworkshop.org.

Chapter 14

1. Steven Galloway, *The Cellist of Sarajevo* (New York: Riverhead Books, 1995).

2. David James Duncan, *God Laughs and Plays* (Great Barrington, MA: Triad Books, 2006).

Chapter 15

1. Henri Nouwen, *The Return of the Prodigal Son* (New York: Doubleday, 1994).

2. Henri Nouwen, *The Essential Henri Nouwen*, ed. Robert A. Jonas (Boston: Shambhala Publications, 2009).

Chapter 16

1. Christine A. Colon and Bonnie E. Field, *Singled Out: Why Celibacy Must Be Reinvented in Today's Church* (Grand Rapids, MI: Brazo Press, 2009).

2. Gregory Boyle, *Tattoos on the Heart: The Power of Boundless Compassion* (New York: Free, 2010).

3. From Mother Teresa's essay for the Architects of Peace Project, which can be found at http://www.scu.edu/ethics/architects-of-peace/Teresa/essay.html.

4. Shane Claiborne, *The Irresistible Revolution: Living as an Ordinary Radical* (Grand Rapids, MI: Zondervan, 2006).

5. Boyle, *Tattoos on the Heart.*

6. Frederick Buechner, *Now and Then: A Memoir of Vocation* (New York: HarperCollins, 1983).

Chapter 17

1. David Janzen, *The Intentional Christian Community Handbook* (Brewster, MA: Paraclete Press, 2013). This is an excellent resource if you want to learn more about living in Christian community.

Chapter 20

1. Gene Edwards, *The Divine Romance* (Wheaton, IL: Tyndale House Publishers, 1992).

2. Kate Hurley, "Mary's Song," not yet recorded.

3. Henri Nouwen, *Seeds of Hope*, ed. Robert Durback (New York: Doubleday, 1997).

4. Edwards, *The Divine Romance,* 227-29.

Thank You...

First of all, I want to thank my team from Harvest House. Terry Glaspey, you have been a godsend. Thank you for believing in this project so much and for allowing me to see for the first time that writing was never meant to be a little side hobby for me. I want to thank my two editors, Laurie Thornton (on the original self-published book) and Kathleen Kerr. Both times through the editing process I didn't feel like I was doing a painful edit, I felt like I was talking to a good friend. So much more fun that way!

I want to thank my wonderful tough-love counselor, Dana Robinson. It would have been fair for me to put you as a coauthor of my book since so much of the wisdom on these pages came from you. Thank you for guiding me so well through the last five years. (To check out Dana's absolutely beautiful reflection and renewal center, go to thedesertsanctuary.com.)

To Mom and Dennis, Shawn and Celeste, Will and Marie, Neal, Kai, Dax, Ariel, Jeremiah, Arowyn, and my sweet sweet John Mark. We went through a lot this year and I am glad you are my family.

To my dear friend Becca Bundy, for being a sounding board for this book and for listening to so much of the pain and joy that are depicted in these pages. Seven years and I can't think of one time that I didn't love being around you.

To the many women in my life who have brought joy and purpose to me. Aimee Herring Brewer, Kate Kemp, Shauna Lott, Dee Butcher (one of the most faithful people I know), Emily Malloure,

Joanna Howard, Sanyu Majola, Andrea Weeks, all my High School Girls, the Tetrapees. Special thanks to Shauna for brainstorming with me on the cover.

To Aaron Strumpel (aaronstrumpel.com) for walking with me through so many journeys and for globetrotting the world with me. You are a good friend.

To the Louisville Pirate Bikers: Trace, Matteo, Kelsey, Kelly, Casandra, Glad and Scotty, Jenny, Aaron, and Trung. Over the years you have brought me so much happiness and so many Irish drinking songs.

To Carson Stitt: I want to live a better life because of the way you live yours. You have inspired me so deeply, beyond words.

To the whole Stitt and Nilles family (including Collin and Avie!) for accepting me as family when most people would have politely asked me to leave.

To Roger: You always make me laugh so hard and I miss you!

To Access, especially Ryan Taylor: you have brought so much depth to this season of my life. Thank you.

To Origins Community: I love you all so much. There is no place I'd rather be on a Sunday night than with you.

To Luke Flowers (lukeflowers.com) for always doing such an amazing job with my artwork and for being a wonderful encouragement every time.

To the many organizations that have challenged me to live a life beyond myself, especially InnerChange (innerchange.org), iempathize (iempathize.org), AIDchild (aidchild.org), and Love146 (love146.com).

This book is dedicated to my father, Mark Hurley. You were a good papa and I miss you.

About the Author

Kate Hurley was a touring singer songwriter and worship leader for 12 years. She's been a featured artist on many albums including *Enter the Worship Circle* and *Absolute Worship* and has recorded six solo albums. She's played and spoken all over the world, from castles in Germany to poor villages in India.

Kate now teaches music lessons, writes, and life coaches in Asheville, North Carolina. She has started a sponsorship program that will allow low income youth to receive free music lessons from her.

Kate travels often to speak at events and share her music. She loves giving retreats for singles, as well as women's retreats. She is working on her next book on the topic of self-compassion and thought life called *Prodigal Mind*. You can read more of her writing at www.resilientblog.org.

You can find her music on iTunes and Spotify. You can contact her via her website, www.katehurley.com, for life coaching, speaking at events, retreats, and house concerts, or sponsoring a student.

She prays that her life and art, including this book, will touch many people with encouragement, hope, and healing.

To learn more about Harvest House books and
to read sample chapters, visit our website:

www.harvesthousepublishers.com

HARVEST HOUSE PUBLISHERS
EUGENE, OREGON